Iniquity

Ana Mendez Ferrell

E & A INTERNATIONAL

Iniquity
1st Edition

All scripture quotations unless otherwise indicated are taken from the King James Version.

Cover design:
Ruben Mariaca Asport
areyou_ben@hotmail.com

Interior production:
*osprey*design
www.ospreydesign.com

Printing:
United Graphics, Inc.

Category:
Deliverance

Publisher:
E & A INTERNATIONAL
P.O. Box 3418
Ponte Vedra Florida 32004
www.anamendez.com

ISBN: 1-933163-08-9

Dedication

I dedicate this book to my beloved, heavenly Father, to Jesus Christ, my Redeemer, and to the Holy Spirit. I also dedicate it to my beloved sisters, my twin, Mercedes Méndez, and Cecilia Pezet, along with my nephews, Santiago and Pablo.

Table of Contents

Introduction   *vii*

1. What Is Iniquity   *1*

2. The Conflict Between
   Two Seeds   *19*

3. True Righteousness Frees Us
   From Iniquity   *29*

4. The Operation and Manifestation
   of Iniquity   *55*

5. The Power of Attraction of
   Spiritual Forces   *93*

   Conclusion: How Do We Deal
   with Iniquity   *101*

Introduction

I am greatly weighed down within my soul as I observe thousands and hundreds of thousands of Christians greatly suffering, going through never-ending deserts, sicknesses with no apparent relief from curses. This suffering has caused me to intensely seek God's face in order to find an answer to so many unanswerable questions.

For many years, God has raised me as a pioneer in a number of areas, one of them being spiritual warfare at the personal deliverance level as well as the territorial level. Invading these terrains and standing against the powers of darkness has allowed me to comprehend God's righteousness in a deeper way. The only force that destroys the power of the devil is the righteousness manifested on the cross of Calvary. This event is much greater than the simple "justification by grace" preached in most churches.

Through this study, God wants us to discover the wonderful treasures hidden in Christ Jesus and, enter the fullness of life only be found through the depth and mysteries of the cross. God not only wants us to understand "iniquity", which is one of the greatest obstacles to possess the riches of His glory, but to be free. He wants us to understand that a lack of knowledge of this topic will doom us to failure and keep us bound to curses from which there is no escape.

In His Word, God makes a specific distinction between sin and iniquity. The Church deals with the topic of sin, to some degree but almost never touches the vast problem of iniquity. The majority of Christians is unaware of its existence much less fight it. Nevertheless, iniquity is a most relevant topic in the Bible, and lack of knowledge or understanding in this area is the greatest source of failure, oppression, defeat and obstacles, which the people of God face.

1

What is Iniquity?

Etymologically this word means, "that which is twisted." Iniquity is, in fact, anything that turns away from God's straight and perfect path.

The origin of iniquity was found in the fall of Lucifer. It occurred the moment this archangel, full of beauty and perfection, permitted a thought that was out of line with God. He then began to believe in something other than what was divine and righteous. Now, just as faith is the "substance" of what is believed and is the power that activates the invisible world of the heavens, this twisted thought inside of this archangel also produced a spiritual substance, which is the origin of evil.

> Thou wast perfect in thy ways from the day that thou wast created, till iniquity was found in thee.
>
> *Ezekiel 28:15*

The Bible then says:

By your many sins and dishonest trade you have desecrated your sanctuaries.

Ezekiel 28:18
(New International Version)

The words iniquity and evil, many times used interchangeably, are fundamental to understand the root of the vast majority of problems we suffer.

Evil is the diabolic seed from which all wickedness originates, it is then transmitted to man in birth, impregnating his heart with thoughts and intentions opposed to righteousness, truth, love and everything God is. Iniquity is the thoughts that are twisted or the sum total of all that is evil in mankind.

Iniquity impregnates the spirit of the human being on conception. In that very instant all of the spiritual data, or the spiritual inheritance of evil is established in this person.

Iniquity operates as a "spiritual or an umbilical cord," that transmits the spiritual DNA of evil from one generation to the next. This is how the twisted, sinful legacy of man is imprinted and passed on to his children. These children in turn will twist it further by their sins, and pass it as a baton of curses to the subsequent generation.

The sin of Judah is written with a pen of iron, and with the point of a diamond: it is graven upon the table of their heart.

Jeremiah 17:1

Iniquity is what the Bible calls the body of sin. As we continue our study, we will see how iniquity has formed part of the spiritual body within man, affecting his behavior, the foundation of his thought process and even the health of his physical body.

The body of sin originates in the spirit and invades the soul and body, like mud that soils everything it touches.

Iniquity is intrinsically tied to the spiritual world of darkness, and it is there the devil binds our curses from our ancestors. It is in this place the legal basis of sickness is rooted from the parents to their children and transmitted to their grandchildren. This is where Satan's legal right is granted to rob, destroy and even kill us. Our Iniquity prevents us from receiving the fullness of the blessings of God.

This is the door the devil has to a human being's life, believer or unbeliever. It is by iniquity the "evil one" permeates the heart of man in order to inflict all kinds of perverse, sinful desires called lust. The inheritance of evil has been transmitted, and has constructed the soul for sin. This is an irresistible force compelling good people to commit abominable sins.

This is why sons of alcoholics, after reaching a certain age, have uncontrollable desires to drink. And sometimes, these are sons of Christians or pastors whom, without any apparent reason whatsoever, begin to develop these sinful inclinations. The reason is iniquity has not been uprooted.

But every man is tempted, when he is drawn away
of his own lust, and enticed. Then when lust hath

conceived, it bringeth forth sin: and sin, when it is finished, bringeth forth death.

James 1:14-15

The devil is not the only one who interferes with the life of a man through iniquity, but God also judges iniquity. Iniquity opposes divine righteousness; and will cause continual friction with God. Righteousness as part of its essence judges anything that is opposite. The purpose for the judgments of God is to order everything with the will and the righteousness of God. If paths are twisted, judgment as a continual divine action will bring tests, tribulations, etc., in an effort to pull the person back to His divine order.

...For I the LORD thy God am a jealous God, visiting the iniquity of the fathers upon the children unto the third and fourth generation of them that hate me.

Exodus 20:5b

Please note He is not talking to unbelievers, but to God's people, and sin is not visited, but iniquity. Sin is the fruit of iniquity. It is the superficial, visible part of something deeply rooted in the human being. Sin can be described as the branches, the exterior of a large tree growing and thriving from generation to generation. Iniquity in this illustration is the root, and it is there we need to apply the ax.

The vast majority of believers confesses their sins to God, but never ask Him to blot out their iniquities. This is why they continue suffering the consequences such as financial curses, incurable family sicknesses, divorces, accidents and tragedies that would never occur with the protection of an omnipotent God.

God Differentiates Between Iniquity and Sin

As I said before, the fruit is not the same as the root. The origin is different from what is visible. Jesus not only came to conquer the sin in our lives, but to destroy all the works of the devil.

When Moses calls out to God to see His glory, the Lord manifests Himself to him and says:

> The LORD, The LORD God, merciful and gracious, longsuffering, and abundant in goodness and truth, keeping mercy for thousands, forgiving iniquity and transgression and sin, and that will by no means clear the guilty.
>
> *Exodus 34:6b-7a*

A principle we must understand, as a source of great liberation in our lives is God does not deal with evil in a generic manner. He is extremely specific, and we must respond the same way to the kingdom of darkness.

One of the tragedies I see in the body of Christ is how people conform to general prayers. For example, "Lord, forgive all of my sins" or "Lord, forgive me for anything that I have done in the past" or perhaps "Lord, forgive me for all sexual sin." Although God hears the intention of our heart and forgives us as far as our eternal salvation is concerned, the legal bases in operation are unaffected with generic prayers.

God wants us to search our hearts and understand evil and its consequences in the same dimension He does. He doesn't want the devil to have even the smallest thing with which to attack us. Jesus died for our complete and total deliverance. His Passion and every part of the cross was and is a specific design to enter into complete fulfillment with Him. He not only paid the price for the forgiveness of our sins, but the cross represents a total work in which each part of our spirit, soul and body were redeemed.

> Surely he hath borne our griefs, and carried our sorrows... But he was wounded for our transgressions; he was bruised for our iniquities: the chastisement of our peace was upon him; and with his stripes we are healed... Yet it pleased the LORD to bruise him; he hath put him to grief: when thou shalt make his soul an offering for sin, he shall see his seed, he shall prolong his days, and the pleasure of the LORD shall prosper in his hand. He shall see of the travail of his soul, and shall be satisfied: by his knowledge shall my righteous servant justify many; for he shall bear their iniquities.
>
> *Isaiah 53:4a-5, 10-11*

In this passage of Isaiah, we see His sacrifice on the cross touching areas in which we must be set free.

A large part of the body of Christ limits itself to receiving salvation from their sins, but their lives are not free from emotional and physical pain. They are trapped in prisons of the soul and spirit, and above all, suffer the burden of carrying their iniquity. Jesus did a complete work in order for us to live a life of fullness in Him. We will never see His total triumph in our lives if we don't understand that we have settled for less than the absolute victory the cross-purchased for us in spirit, soul and body.

We clearly see God differentiates between iniquity and sin, in the ceremony of expiation of the Old Testament, a type and shadow of Jesus at Calvary.

> And Aaron shall lay both his hands upon the head of the live goat, and confess over him all the iniquities of the children of Israel, and all their transgressions and all their sins, putting them upon the head of the goat, and shall send him away by the hand of a fit man into the wilderness.
>
> *Leviticus 16:21*

God is specifically cleansing His people through a detailed revelation of the three corrupt forms of the human condition.

Iniquity, Part of Man's Spirit
Man Is Comprised of Spirit, Soul and Body

The human beings are extremely complex, and at the same time wonderful, living machinery. A study of the systems and organs of our body evokes in us wonder and amazement at the work of God.

Of the three parts of our being, spirit, soul and body, the easiest to understand is the body. However, it has taken hundreds of years for medical science to comprehend, and even now, there remains many unsolved mysteries.

Man must be understood as a whole, combining the three parts of his makeup. Leaving one of them out leads to error. Science cannot comprehend the ties between the body and the spirit, because the latter is totally unknown to them.

The body, as we know, is comprised of innumerable components to function properly. In the same way, the soul and spirit are complex, invisible bodies necessary to understand in order to receive the victory won for us by Jesus. The failure for millions of Christians is in large part a result of this lack of knowledge of these two fundamental parts of our being.

Some theologies teach the soul is comprised of the mind, will and emotions, and the spirit makeup is communion, intuition and conscience. The soul and spirit represent two enormous areas of virtually unknown territory, the depths of which most Christians ignore in order to escape complications. Unfortunately, this attitude keeps millions of people bound to deserts and tribulations from which they cannot escape.

Others more versed in the study of these areas, in an attempt to explain the demonic oppression of believers compare the triune man with the tabernacle of Moses. They compare the body as the outer court, the soul as the "holy place" and the spirit as the "holy of holies". Using this model, a Christian can be bound or oppressed by demons in his body, the same way unholy people entered into the outer courts of the temple. This illustration explains the spirits of sickness afflicting the physical body.

They conclude that demon spirits are free to afflict the soul. These are demons such as fear, depression, wrath, etc. However, the spirit of man can only be possessed either by God or by the devil. Once the Holy Spirit seals a man's spirit, he is absolutely pure. From this point, the problem lies only in the soul and body.

I believe God is taking us to a deeper investigation of the places in the spirit not yet revealed.

Describing the spirit as a combination of three parts, communion, intuition and conscience, would be the same as teaching that the human body is only the head, trunk and extremities.

Paul mentions in his first letter to the Corinthians that there is a natural body and a spiritual body (1 Corinthians 15:44). Both are made of a complexity of organs and systems connecting one another. These systems allow the body to function in its own dimension, the physical body in the material world, and the spiritual body in the spiritual arena, even though they are linked together.

My understanding differs from the belief that the spirit is pure because God dwells there. I will cite a few texts from the Bible to support my belief:

> Having therefore these promises, dearly beloved, let us cleanse ourselves from all filthiness of the flesh and spirit, perfecting holiness in the fear of God.
>
> *2 Corinthians 7:1*

> And the very God of peace sanctify you wholly; and I pray God your whole spirit and soul and body be

preserved blameless unto the coming of our Lord Jesus Christ.

1 Thessalonians 5:23

These verses contend there is a spiritual contamination from which we must be cleansed, and God demands sanctification in all three parts of our being.

Without an exhaustive study of what the spirit is, which would take an entire book; let's observe our spirit's make-up and some of its different parts.

Parts of the Spirit
Communion

This part of our spirit is united with God, through the seed of His Son implanted within us. This is the organ that determines if a spirit is alive or dead in relation to God.

This is one of the components in which God's voice is heard with clarity. It is the place of glorious intimacy in which we feel we are one with the Holy Spirit. It is in this area the lordship of Jesus Christ is established, and directs our lives. This is where the visions and revelations from the Spirit of God manifest in visible form.

Communion is the central part of the spiritual body, and is the "holy of holies" of our temple. This place is possessed by the prince of darkness, if one has not come to Christ. This is what the Word says:

> To open their eyes (of the unbelievers), and to turn them from darkness to light, and from the power of Satan unto God...

Acts 26:18a

Heaven and Earth converge in man when we surrender our lordship to His Lordship. This is how the kingdom of God is established in our midst. Through communion we see and penetrate the spiritual world. God can transform us into His image and even gives us the hidden treasures of His Glory.

The life of God is conceived in this region, beginning with the new birth and eventually a new creature. Regeneration starts here, and makes us alive by the Spirit of resurrection.

Communion is connected to other parts of our spirit, and functions as the governing place of our spiritual being. Like the heart it is the very marrow of the inner man.

Communion also is one of the parts the spirit uses to communicate with the soul, specifically with the heart and the emotions.

The Bible says:

Keep your heart with all vigilance and above all that you guard, for out of it flows the springs of life.

Proverbs 4:23
(The Amplified Bible)

Intuition

Although this word is not biblical, it is recognized by the dictionary and by some theologians as part of the spirit.

Intuition represents the antennas connecting the natural world to the spiritual world. It makes us aware of demonic angelic spirits. Sometimes we feel as though someone is observing us or we are being followed.. This is intuition detecting the spiritual world as type of cosmic radar.

We are aware something is a certain way, with no logical explanation; such as a strong feeling, someone will call. We can simply know a loved one far away is all right or something is wrong

In my experience organizing events for the ministry, I can sense formation of hindrances taking place in the spiritual realm trying to prevent the success of our planning. As a result, this urges me to seek the Lord for the reason for the obstruction.

Sometimes we know the results of an interview before it happens or, we detect someone has the intentions of betraying us. Perhaps the words or actions of a person have the appearance of righteousness, but something in our spirit warns us about the danger.

Intuition receives revelation from God. Many prophetic words given in personal form emanate from this part of our spirit. Gifts of the Holy Ghost such as words of knowledge as well as prophecy are manifested from this part of our spirit.

Conscience

This part of our spirit is where the fear of God and the wisdom of God reside. It is the place in which our being knows the difference between right and wrong without ever having read the Bible.

> For when the Gentiles, which have not the law, do by nature the things contained in the law, these, having not the law, are a law unto themselves: which show the work of the law written in their hearts, their conscience also bearing witness, and their thoughts the

mean while accusing or else excusing one another;) in the day when God shall judge the secrets of men by Jesus Christ according to my gospel.

Romans 2:14-16

Conscience, communion and other parts of the spirit are intimately tied to the heart of man. The unrenewed mind, together with its reasoning, are conformed to this world. Many times, this is why the reasoning of the heart differs from that of the mind. This is the part of the spirit awakened when man ate of the knowledge of good and evil.

If man continually sins, that part of God connected to his conscience, called the "fear of God", is separated. This causes the conscience to harden, becoming more insensitive to the will of God, ultimately producing the "hardening of the heart."

Now the Spirit speaketh expressly, that in the latter times some shall depart from the faith, giving heed to seducing spirits, and doctrines of devils; speaking lies in hypocrisy; having their conscience seared with a hot iron; forbidding to marry, and commanding to abstain from meats, which God hath created...

1 Timothy 4:1-3a

The Mind of the Spirit

The mind of the spirit is made of various parts: understanding, spiritual intelligence and wisdom of God. The mind of the spirit is where the knowledge of God rests. One can supernaturally receive knowledge of things about God never been taught. This part of the spirit receives the mind of Christ, illuminating and permitting us to understand and comprehend. God reveals the great mysteries of science to the righteous as well as the unjust. Paul prays for the eyes of their spiritual understanding to be opened for them to understand the riches of His glory.

> That the God of our Lord Jesus Christ, the Father of glory, may give unto you the spirit of wisdom and revelation in the knowledge of him: the eyes of your understanding being enlightened; that ye may know what is the hope of his calling, and what the riches of the glory of his inheritance in the saints, and what is the exceeding greatness of his power to us-ward who believe, according to the working of his mighty power, which he wrought in Christ, when he raise him form the dead, and set his own right hand in the heavenly places.

> *Ephesians 1:17-20*

In this scripture Paul prays to awake and activate different parts of our spirit. The knowledge of God penetrates out intuition while the eyes of out understanding bring light to the mind of the spirit. The area of out spiritual inheritance, which will be discussed later, is the location of our spiritual genetics. The power of His Resurrection I believe resides in a place I call the seat of His power.

Spirituals Senses

The same way, we have physical senses in the natural world, we have spirituals ones in order to relate to the invisible world. These help us detect the origin of the words impacting our spirit. This is known as spiritual discernment.

> But strong meat belongeth to them that are of full age, even those who by reason of use have their senses exercised to discern both good and evil.

Hebrews 6:6

Every human spirit can see, hear, hear, smell, taste and touch. Visions and ecstasies are observed through our spiritual eyes. All spiritual voices are transmitted through our spiritual ears. Johns' experience in heaven illustrates the book that was sweet in his mouth and bitter in his stomach.

> And I went unto the angel, and said unto him, Give me the little book. And he said unto me, Take it, and eat it up; and it shall make thy belly bitter, but it shall be in they mouth sweet as honey. And I took the little book out of the angel's hand, and ate it up; and it was in my mouth sweet as honey: and as soon as I had eaten it, my belly was bitter.

Rev 10:9-10

Spiritual touch, perhaps the most developed sense within us, is the sensations of the Holy Spirit, or feeling of God embracing us. Many times during spiritual warfare, one can feel the spirit of death as coldness throughout ones body even though the climate may be warm. Some times, a developed spirit will perceive spiritual fragrances, such as aromas coming from the presence of God, or the stench of unclean spirits.

The senses of the spirit are connected to the senses of the soul, and complement one another.

The Seat of Power

Our spirit possesses an area where the power of God resides. It is through this part of our spirit that the gifts of miracles, healings and wonders of God are manifested. This is the engine of the spirit. This is the place Samson received his strength. This was the origin of power residing in Moses' hand, and staff, and parted the Red Sea. We are the extension of God's hands. As the prophet Habakkuk said:

> And his brightness was as the light; he had horns coming out of his hand: and there was the hiding of his power.
>
> *Habakkuk 3:4*

Paul said:

> Now unto him that is able to do exceeding abundantly above all that we ask or think, according to the power that worketh in us.
>
> *Ephesians 3:20*

The apostles received the Spirit of God when Jesus blew on them before his ascension. However, he told them,

> But ye shall receive power, after that the Holy Ghost is come upon you: and ye shall be witnesses unto me

both in Jerusalem, and in all Judea, and in Samaria, and unto the uttermost part of the earth.

Acts 1:8

This illustrates the Holy Spirit can fill us in many areas of the spirit, activating each one, until arriving at spiritual fullness. We observe believers in whom one part of their spirit is much more developed than others. There are prophetic believers with intuition, but who are ineffective in the areas of power. The gifts of the Spirit manifest in different parts of our spiritual being, developing that area corresponding with each gift.

There is a principle at work that states as it is in the natural realm, so it is in the spiritual. Just as with our physical existence, we have natural gifts that are manifested in different areas of the soul and body, so it is with the spiritual body. Some people develop their mental gifts, in science, language and other professions. Many are inclined towards the arts and sports; others develop a combination of them all.

Inheritance

Our material body stores genetic information in the chromosomes of the cell. These chromosomes resemble a transparent cord called DNA, where all of the data of our physical inheritance is found. Similar to a microchip in a computer, all our software or building blocks are located in this transparent cord. It is the DNA that determines if we are born with features resembling our grandfather's eyes, mother's mouth, hair color of our great-grandfather, or the height of our father. All of this information is transmitted from generation to generation. When the cells of the embryo multiply within the mother's womb, a body is created and designed according to this information.

This same model is found in the spiritual body. This spiritual DNA is similar to an invisible scorecard in recording information from generation to generation. This information is called iniquity.

God provided us a redeemed inheritance, in the Spirit of Christ, which must dominate our cursed inheritance. Unfortunately, because this topic is rarely mentioned in the Church, continue to suffer the consequences from this part of their spirit.

God Himself attributes to the spirit of man the responsibility of his own evil:

> For the LORD, the God of Israel saith that he hateth putting away: for one covereth violence with his garment, saith the LORD of hosts: therefore take heed to your spirit that ye deal not treacherously.
>
> *Malachi 2:16*

This book is not an exhaustive study on our spirit. However, I believe it is important to understand it as much as possible in a general sense, so as to realize some key characteristics of our being. These keys can be critical to unlock the liberty obtained for us through Christ Jesus.

2

The Conflict Between Two Seeds

Iniquity is the Body of Sin

We have discovered iniquity to be a demonic seed, conceived in the spirit of man, which is responsible for the sinful activity committed during his lifetime.

The Bible talks about two seeds in conflict with another one.

And I will put enmity between thee and the woman, and between thy seed and her seed; it shall bruise thy head, and thou shalt bruise his heel.

Genesis 3:15

These seeds represent two natures, one demonic, and the other divine. This is the seed of promise made to Abraham by God.

Now to Abraham and his seed were the promises made. He saith not, and to seeds, as of many; but as of one, and to thy seed, which is Christ.

Galatians 3:16

This divine seed is conceived in our spirit, if we submit to Christ, and accept what He did for us on the cross. In that moment, there begins an internal conflict between our "flesh" or unrenewed soul, and the divine seed just planted. The flesh will be nourished with iniquity and will fight to prevail. The life of Christ will struggle with the flesh, and provoke us to live by the Spirit.

What is the flesh? This is the building the devil constructs in our souls using the blocks of iniquity. From birth, iniquity is implanted in our spirit and begins to contaminate our heart, reasoning, and even what we believe about ourselves.

The flesh is a complex structure. It is our home as fallen beings. It is the manifestation of our spiritual inheritance through the work of iniquity. The devil turns us from the divine righteousness of God, to destroy us through selfishness and pride.

Do ye indeed speak righteousness, O congregation? Do ye judge uprightly, O ye sons of men? Yea, in heart ye work wickedness; ye weigh the violence of your hands in the earth. The wicked are estranged from the womb: they go astray as soon as they be born, speaking lies.

Psalm 58:1-3

King David recognized this internal conflict that propelled him toward evil, even causing him to fall into adultery with Bathsheba. He had a clear understanding of what had happened to him and prays about the root of the problem. The light of the Most High shows him the difference between iniquity, rebellion and sin. He understood the reason for his sinful behavior, so he writes:

Have mercy upon me, O God, according to thy lovingkindness: according unto the multitude of thy tender mercies blot out my transgressions. Wash me thoroughly from mine iniquity, and cleanse me from my sin. For I acknowledge my transgressions: and my sin is ever before me. Against thee, thee only, have I sinned, and done this evil in thy sight: that thou mightest be justified when thou speakest, and be clear when thou judgest. Behold, I was shapen in iniquity, and in sin did my mother conceive me. Behold, thou desirest truth in the inward parts: and in the hidden part thou shalt make me to know wisdom.

Psalm 51:1-6

We observe that iniquity is implanted at birth, and if not purged from our being, will make us enemies of God.

These two seeds remain in conflict with one another until one of the two dies. If iniquity is not destroyed it will permit more than mere internal struggle, as we will see later on.

Iniquity is from the spirit of man. The flesh receives its power and nourishment from this structure. Iniquity manifests itself in the soul, creating a dense veil impeding the development of any spiritual life. It is the force that imprisons us in our mind and heart, making us depend on our ways of thinking than those of God.

The flesh is the manifestation of iniquity as illustrated in Galatians 5:

> Now the works of the flesh are manifest, which are these; Adultery, fornication, uncleanness, lasciviousness, idolatry, witchcraft, hatred, variance, emulations, wrath, strife, seditions, heresies, envying, murders, drunkenness, revellings, and such like: of the which I tell you before, as I have also told you in time past, that they which do such things shall not inherit the kingdom of God.
>
> *Galatians 5:19-21*

These are just fruit, external evidence of a structure, habits and paradigms that have controlled our life for years and are only destroyed with the power of the Spirit. Eliminating the fruit is merely an external work. One example is an alcoholic who receives Christ and stops drinking. If he never confronts the roots of pain, bitterness, and rebellion that controlled him, inevitably, iniquity the power behind the sin will compel him to other sinful behavior. His heart has recorded, "You must escape. You can't handle the pain." This decree, by the man is nourished by iniquity and relentlessly pressures his flesh. He will eventually spiral into a life of lies, adultery or escape into cyber pornography. This person believes he has been free from alcohol, but in reality, all he did was to cut one visible fruit. He has never gone to the root of the problem.

Pruning the superficial part or the visible sin is just an attempt at our sanctification, but that's not all we need. This is why there is so much frustration, condemnation and hypocrisy in our Churches. God wants us illuminated in our understanding to obtain our true inheritance: the abundant life purchased by Jesus.

While praying intensely, God revealed to me that very few of His people understand what it means to walk in the Spirit. This type of life is not found in going to church every Sunday or even every day, or memorizing the Bible or serving in a church. Walking in the Spirit will develop each area of our spiritual being. It is a supernatural walk, totally led by the Spirit of God. It is the visible manifestation of Christ in us and the total destruction of the body of sin that is iniquity.

THE WILL OF MAN DOES NOT DESTROY THE WORKS OF THE FLESH; THE SPIRIT OF GOD DOES. It is the seed of God destroying the demonic seed in the flesh. This is only accomplished by the life of the Spirit and spending intimate time with God.

The flesh disguises itself in spirituality. In doing so attracts horrendous religious spirits. Religion controls the flesh. Religion is only concerned with external habits, which appears righteous. Religion, with its rules and legalism, cannot affect the internal part of our being. This is only achieved when our spirit becomes His Spirit.

The religious man enjoys DOING visibly pious things. However, that which is of the Spirit has nothing in common with DOING, but with BEING. This is vitally important. We must understand efforts and sacrifices accomplish little, if not led by the Spirit. We will become disgusted with anything that has to do with church. This is why we find many worn out servants of God, without strength and unsure what else they should do or in which direction to go.

The devil's plan is to permeate the Holy Church of Jesus Christ with religiosity, to control it by iniquity, thus killing the life of the Spirit.

Ministering to the heart of God must be done by the leading of the Holy Spirit. Most Churches follow a program that includes reading scriptures, praying and singing but without the leading of the Spirit of God. Doing things in this manner is the result of iniquity and it has hindered our spiritual development and true relationship with the Lord.

In the vast majority of churches, there is little or no emphasis on worshiping in the depth of the Spirit, allowing the genuine flow of intimacy with God. This is what equips the believers in their spiritual progress.

There is such a tendency to give priority to men's programs, instead of liberty to God. This has produced a carnal Christianity (humanly structured) that lacks spiritual efficacy in the majority of the members of the church.

It is relatively easy to create a religious system of rules and formulas that everyone can follow. Many are afraid to enter the unknown ways of the Spirit, because they no longer control what happens or can explain it with human words. It is easier to eliminate the things of the Spirit, which we don't understand, and manage the familiar. Unfortunately, this attitude has invaded the church, making the church for the most part ineffective, powerless and dead.

However, God is once again knocking at our door, in order for us to understand truths in a new way. He desires to fill us with His power, wisdom and might, and will do so in those who truly crucify their flesh.

And they that are Christ's have crucified the flesh with the affections and lusts.

Galatians 5:24

The flesh, intimately tied to iniquity, serves the law of sin and death and is opposed to the life of the spirit.

In the book to the Romans, we see the struggle between the two seeds. The results of this struggle will determine our final destiny.

There is therefore now no condemnation to them which are in Christ Jesus, who walk not after the flesh, but after the Spirit. For THE LAW OF THE SPIRIT OF LIFE in Christ Jesus hath made me free from THE LAW OF SIN AND DEATH.

Romans 8:1-2

Note in this passage God makes clear there is no condemnation for those who walk according to the Spirit. It does not say there is no condemnation for those who say, "Lord, Lord," but only those who do not walk according to the flesh. After all, the apostle mentions two laws, which oppose one another: that of the spirit, governed by Christ, and the law of sin and death, operated by the devil through iniquity.

As long as iniquity is not eradicated, the believer will be imprisoned in the flesh. On one hand, the believer will attempt to live a spiritual life, because he loves Jesus, but inevitably will form fleshly conclusions. Decisions will be made according to his mind and emotions. Most times his opinion on spiritual matters is controlled by religious thoughts, which result in his slow development. He will be negative. His faith will be high and low, or even nonexistent. Iniquity will create feelings of guilt, fear and preoccupation with death.

The objective of iniquity is for us to remain focused on this world. It is the enemy of the cross. I have received invitations to preach in which I have been specifically forbidden to talk about the cross, or anything else that might disturb the comfort of the Church. Obviously, I did not or will not accept such invitations.

It is taught in many seminaries in order to have a large church, one should speak as little as possible about the cross and sin. Many ministers are trapped by iniquity having the appearance of spirituality, but seeking the fame OF THIS WORLD through large world ministries. They desire the recognition of great ministries and the favor of men. When the preaching of the Word and the liberty of the Spirit are compromised, iniquity manifests in the fear of man more than on the fear of God.

> Brethren, be followers together of me, and mark them which walk so as ye have us for an ensample. (For many walk, of whom I have told you often, and now tell you even weeping, that they are the enemies of the cross of Christ: whose end is destruction, whose

God is their belly, and whose glory is in their shame, who mind earthly things.)

The spiritual man is satisfied when God is pleased. If it is a large ministry, great, and if not, that's O.K, too. The most important thing is to do the will of God, even though it implies losing everything in order to please the Father.

For they that are after the flesh do mind the things of the flesh; but they that are after the Spirit the things of the Spirit. For to be carnally minded is death; but to be spiritually minded is life and peace. Because the carnal mind is enmity against God: for it is not subject to the law of God, neither indeed can be.

Romans 8:5-7

One thing clearly Illustrated in the Scriptures is one cannot BE of the Spirit and BE of the flesh at the same time. You are either one or the other.

BEING of the Spirit implies one manner of behavior, and objectives different from those of the world. The theory you can live in the flesh and spirit because the righteousness of God justifies us regardless of what one does, has created a Church filled with sin, sickness, religion and spiritual death. The Church doesn't have the slightest idea what it means to live by the Spirit.

I believe God is calling us to stop and review many doctrines we have accepted and examine them in the light of the results they have produced.

3

True Righteousness Frees
Us From Iniquity

The fundamental principles of faith expounded upon in this chapter, are from a deeper perspective routinely preached today. They are developed from a prophetic and apostolic understanding, capable of supporting His latter-day glory.

1. Righteousness, The Focus of a
New Apostolic Reformation

It is impossible to speak about iniquity and our deliverance, without a clear understanding of the cross of Christ. Inadequate interpretations of this foundational topic, have resulted in millions of people, believing they have obtained salvation when in reality they have not.

God is restoring all things before His return, and one of the most important is the preaching of the true Gospel of Jesus Christ, in all of its power and glory.

I deeply believe in the total work of the cross. It is my life and reason for living. I believe in its absolute justifying, redeeming and healing power. I believe we are saved by grace through faith; a faith producing powerful works in God.

I also believe we have diluted the preaching of the true Gospel in such a way, as to attract people who in many instances, have never understood the basics of salvation. We have reduced a transforming, but at the same time, confronting Gospel to a simple, sweet "sinner's prayer", lacking spiritual reality and commitment. Large numbers of people who pray this prayer don't have the slightest conviction of sin, or the desire to withdraw from the world in order to follow Jesus.

We offer them wonderful promises, instructing them to believe the blessings of God are theirs because God now considers them "righteous", even though their lives are filled with sin and unrighteousness. The vast majority of the church lives in total defeat, never-ending wilderness, calling themselves alive to Christ, but in reality they are dead.

Justification through faith is acquired after I believe with all my heart that Jesus took my sins upon the cross. This requires my life in its totality. Justification occurs as I make the decision to leave my old life and the realization that my deeds crucified Jesus.

Union with Christ is a marriage. In fact, Paul makes this comparison in his epistle to the Galatians. When a man marries, he leaves behind his old way of living as a bachelor, his parent's house and is united by commitment to his wife. The same thing happens when we are united to Christ. We leave behind our old manner of living and are united in one Spirit with the Lord.

Today, in many instances we live a Gospel without commitment. As if the old structure of sin in our lives need not change. Many professing Christians live under the belief that they are justified by grace and that they will enter into the kingdom of heaven, regardless of what they do, because one day they said with their mouth, "Lord, come live in my heart." This is a dangerous lie.

Although grace is the unmerited favor and mercy of God, and salvation does not require man's works, we cannot avoid entering by way of the CROSS.

The cross is not an option; it is the NARROW DOOR that leads to salvation. It is where the REPENTANT heart surrenders its life in order to begin a new life, leaving behind the practice of sin.

> Enter ye in at the strait gate: for wide is the gate, and broad is the way, that leadeth to destruction, and many there be which go in thereat: Because strait is the gate, and narrow is the way, which leadeth unto life, and few there be that find it.
>
> *Matthew 7:13-14*

2. What Does It Mean to Invoke the Name of the Lord?

Invoking the name of Jesus is extremely powerful, but requires an action on our part. To invoke means, "to call inside". This means calling the Spirit of the living God inside us to unite our spirit. This indispensable step in salvation must be in God's order, for our foundation of faith to be true.

> Nevertheless the foundation of God standeth sure, having this seal, The Lord knoweth them that are his. And, Let every one that nameth the name of Christ depart from iniquity.
>
> *2 Timothy 2:19*

This point seems essential to me, so I ask you to open your heart in order to understand this basic truth. A truth treated with too much levity by the church today.

The first thing to understand for the Spirit of God to move upon us is to decide to remove ourselves from iniquity.

Everyone wants to be sealed by the Spirit of promise, but we are only sealed after we invoke in truth the name of Christ. This is not done with a simple prayer, ignorant of His significance, but with an act of conviction. Then we decide wholeheartedly to change our ways, by removing ourselves from iniquity and live in righteousness.

For with the heart man believeth unto righteousness;
and with the mouth confession is made unto salvation.

Romans 10:10

3. You Must Believe with the Heart, Not the Mind

Believing with the heart implies a determination to walk
in the righteousness of God, sustained by His grace in all
the power needed to be conformed in his righteousness.

We cannot say, "I believe in God," and do whatever we
want, because God "calls us righteous". The apostle James
refers to this way of believing as ineffective faith, since it is
not accompanied by works. He says:

Thou believest that there is one God; thou doest well:
the devils also believe, and tremble. But wilt thou
know, O vain man that faith without works is dead?

James 2:19-20

It is in our heart where the belief system of our being is
found. Only our heart has the inner strength to change the
direction of our life. The mind reflects and accepts, but it
lacks the power to break patterns of behavior. The decisions
in our life can only be made with the heart.

Watchman Nee, the famous theologian of the last century
wrote in his book *The Spiritual Man:*

"Everything that belongs to the natural man, such as for
example the self of the believer, should pass through the
death of the cross. If simply an idea or a concept is presented,

perhaps the mind will accept it. However, if it is something that one must put into practice, the mind immediately will reject it." (Volume 2, page 314)

Only the heart can decide to enter through the door of the cross, humiliating oneself, obeying and renouncing the pleasures and rudiments of the world.

Dr. Nee also stated in this same book:

"Many people call themselves Christians, but what they believe is philosophy, ethics and doctrines about the truth or some supernatural phenomena. Believing this way does not produce new birth, or give these people a new spirit." (Volume 2, page 299)

If we believe with only the mind, we can recite the Bible, or "the creed", but none of these things will result in our new birth.

4. We Must Leave Behind the Old, Sinful Way of Living

The apostle John corroborates what we are saying; emphasizing that walking in iniquity and believing you are righteous is a terrible deceit. Remember, iniquity and righteousness radically oppose one another, and if they coexist in the life of a supposed believer, he will find himself in a lamentable state of judgment throughout his entire existence. Because righteousness inevitably judges iniquity.

And ye know that he was manifested to take away our sins; and in him is no sin. Whosoever abideth in him

SINNETH NOT: whosoever sinneth hath not seen him, neither known him. Little children, LET NO MAN DECEIVE YOU: he that doeth righteousness is RIGHTEOUS, even as he is righteous. He that committeth sin is of the devil; for the devil sinneth from the beginning. For this purpose the Son of God was manifested, that he might destroy the works of the devil. Whosoever is born of God doth not commit sin; for his seed remaineth in him: and he cannot sin, because he is born of God. In this the children of God are manifest, and the children of the devil: whosoever doeth not righteousness is not of God, neither he that loveth not his brother.

1 John 3:6-10

A profound effect is made in the heart of a man who has invoked the name of Jesus. Christ is raised in power in order to undo all iniquity and the works of the devil that have been resident in the true believer. John, by understanding the action of the divine seed, knows beyond a doubt what the presence of Christ in the spirit and heart of man do to sin. The devil will not be able to touch a true son of God, with out His permission

We know that whosoever is born of God SINNETH NOT; but he that is begotten of God keepeth himself, and that WICKED ONE TOUCHETH HIM NOT.

1 John 5:18

The Gospel is a call for a true conversion, which literally translates us from the kingdom of darkness to that of light.

When the apostle Paul was converted on the road to Damascus, the Lord spoke very clearly to him about his calling, saying:

...For I have appeared unto thee for this purpose, to make thee a minister and a witness of these things which thou hast seen... delivering thee from the people, and from the Gentiles, unto whom now I send thee, to open their eyes, and to turn them from darkness to light, and from the power of Satan unto God...

Acts 26:16b–18a

The Lord uses this word "turn", implying a change of location. This means one cannot be in two places at the same time. To turn means to change directions. People who want the world and Christ at the same time have never turned, nor resisted the power of Satan.

If we open our eyes and see the condition of our soul in relation to God, we will decide to leave darkness and then we can be CONVERTED to the light.

5. All Who Claim To Be Saved, Are They Really?

The Gospel is the authentic power of God, delivering us from a vain, carnal, sinful way of life, in order to genuinely produces new, powerful creatures in Him, full of His glory.

When God began to release His apostolic anointing upon my life, I began to see things in the Word I had never seen before. The Lord began a reformation inside of me so I could equip His church for His Second Coming. He has instructed me to reread the Bible, reordering truths that previously I had accepted in a pragmatic way as they had been taught to me. I never questioned them until the evidence of a Church, consumed in sin compelled me to search the Scriptures in a new way, because I love it so much.

The seed of God and the life of the Spirit do not mix with iniquity and the practice of sin. I know this, because I am living it.

Today, we (the Church) take those people who recite God's promises but have not truly repented as heirs of salvation. These people want, "the best of both worlds". They want all the blessings of God and all the pleasures of this world. Today the church labels "born again sons of God" fornicators, adulterers, homosexuals, deceivers, thieves, prideful people, pornographers, abusers and liars. Today we use terms such as baptized in the Spirit with those filled with lust and deceit, witchcraft and idolatry.

Know ye not that the unrighteous shall not inherit the kingdom of God? BE NOT DECEIVED: neither fornicators, nor idolaters, nor adulterers, nor effeminate, nor abusers of themselves with mankind, nor thieves, nor covetous, nor drunkards, nor revilers, nor extortioners, shall inherit the kingdom of God.

1 Corinthians 6:9-10

This verse was written by the same apostle Paul who also wrote the most often quoted salvation verse:

For with the heart man believeth unto righteousness; and with the mouth confession is made unto salvation.

Romans 10:10

The Gospel is not a theological position, but a genuine practice of holiness purchased by Jesus for us on the cross. The early church grew in the FEAR OF GOD and His righteousness. They honored what Jesus did, living a life that glorified God.

> And they continued stedfastly in the apostles' doctrine and fellowship, and in breaking of bread, and in prayers. And FEAR came upon every soul...
>
> *Acts 2:42-43a*

It was clear for them; one cannot BE of the flesh and of the Spirit simultaneously, as practiced today in many churches.

Paul makes this distinction very clear as a basic part of the "doctrine of the apostles":

> For what the law could not do, in that it was weak through the flesh, God sending his own Son in the likeness of sinful flesh, and for sin, condemned sin in the flesh: that the RIGHTEOUSNESS of the law MIGHT BE FULFILLED IN US, WHO WALK NOT AFTER THE FLESH, BUT AFTER THE SPIRIT.
>
> *Romans 8:3-4*

True conversion translates the believer to a life in the Spirit. Notice the passage to the Romans just cited, the righteousness of God is fulfilled only after leaving the carnal life of sin, then the believer lives by the Spirit.

When Christ truly enters into the spirit of man, that life will radically change. Christ, living in us, is a spiritual reality that shakes everything inside. It breaks all of the worldly, sinful systems within us. He will take our heart, surround it with his might and will submerge it with His Light. This produces in us a total change in our thinking. Our thirst and hunger will be for the things of heaven. This world will offer nothing to attract us. The seed of life, Him within us, is full of strength, fire and resurrection. It is not just any seed; it is the LIVING GOD WITHIN US.

If God is truly dwelling within someone, that someone cannot remain in a life of sin. Something occurs extremely powerful when the Creator of the Universe enters into the heart of a man or a woman.

> But ye are not in the flesh, but in the Spirit, if so be that the Spirit of God dwell in you. Now if any man have not the Spirit of Christ, he is none of his.
>
> *Romans 8:9*

The apostle Paul says that the evidence of the Spirit of God really inhabiting a person is he lives according to the Spirit. He leaves his sinful ways of living and is led by the Spirit of Christ.

> For as many as are led by the Spirit of God, they are the sons of God.
>
> *Romans 8:14*

Being led by God means hearing His voice, via our conscience, His Word, our dreams or through the prophetic word. Led by God means having the "fear of God", leading us in His ways and commandments.

The powerful Gospel of Jesus Christ is a call to follow Him. It is not a cute little formula or prayer made in ignorance, without commitment.

Salvation lies in man's response to Jesus' sacrifice. Transformation by His power is only through surrendering our life and leaving our former way of life. If this is not the settling in our heart, we have not yet obtained salvation. We may be walking in that direction, but we are not sealed until we totally surrender our life on His cross.

Some follow Him, surrendering their lives in a radical way, through a simple prayer originated from the depths of their being. They are sealed at that moment. Others approach Him little by little, until surrendering their hearts totally in order to receive their salvation. Others may only have the opportunity to pray before dying, and this is enough for God to save them.

The timing as well as the heart of every man is different. We cannot create a formula and expect everyone to fit inside of it.

AND THEY THAT ARE CHRIST'S <u>HAVE</u> CRUCIFIED the flesh with the affections and lusts.

Galatians 5:24

It does not say as is preached today, they are going to crucify their flesh little by little.

Salvation is not only found in Romans 10:8-9, but in a deep understanding of the New Testament. It is part of a series of truths that compliment it and give sustenance, content and form. Using this verse as an isolated prayer in order to obtain "microwave believers" to fill church membership rolls is a monumental error God wants corrected.

God is restoring not only the preaching of His Gospel, but our understanding of the meaning of, "The pearl of great price." The way we live, as the body of Christ should lift up Jesus' Name in honor, as He deserves and not dishonoring His name through all kinds of unrighteousness in our lives.

6. There is a Difference Between a "Sinner" and an Immature Christian

The Bible considers a "sinner" to be someone who practices sin. This means living according to the rudiments and passions of this world. Someone who sins consistently as a way of life, ignoring the sacrifice of Jesus. None of the apostles who wrote the New Testament considered those who practiced sin as one who was "born again" or much less would he is called "Spirit filled."

The Bible makes a difference between being a sinner and being an immature Christian. It is one thing to be a carnal babe in Christ, saying, "I am of Paul; or, I am of Apollos" (1 Corinthians 3:1-7). It is quite another being an adulterer, a thief, a liar or one who consults fortune-tellers.

It is one thing not to have a renewed mind, and being offended at someone who hurts you, and quite another is lying, fraud or watching pornography on the Internet. All sin defiles the soul and spirit; but there are sins of death and sins of immaturity.

If any man sees his brother sin a sin which is not unto death, he shall ask, and he shall give him life for them that sin not unto death. There is a sin unto death: I do not say that he shall pray for it. All unrighteousness is sin: and there is a sin not unto death. We know that whosoever is born of God sinneth not; but he that is begotten of God keepeth himself, and that wicked one toucheth him not.

1 John 5:16-18

There are theologians who suggest this passage refers to blaspheming the Holy Spirit. However, in the context of this letter, John does not mention that topic. In this manuscript of the apostle is the deep revelation he has regarding those who are sons of God and those who are not. Throughout his epistle, he repeatedly touches on the importance of not practicing sin. This is why I believe John defines the "sin unto death" the Law of Moses.

Keeping oneself holy, without practicing sin, is not being legalistic or "living according to the law". It means "living according to the Spirit" and being directed by the Spirit of God.

Jesus Himself said:

Think not that I am come to destroy the law, or the prophets: I am not come to destroy, but to fulfil.... For I say unto you, that except your righteousness shall exceed the righteousness of the scribes and Pharisees, ye shall in no case enter into the kingdom of heaven.

Matthew 5:17 and 20

I am not saying we can't trip and sin. The Word puts it well:

> ...And if any man sin, we have an advocate with the Father, Jesus Christ the righteous.

1 John 2:1

I am referring to the life of people who call themselves Christians, and yet continue loving the world and practicing sin. They believe they will go to heaven by grace, while they have never had a true encounter with the sacrifice of Christ in their own lives. They believe that they are saved because of repeating a prayer someone had them repeat.

Look at how Paul differentiates between a "sinner" and a "carnal or immature Christian". Reading with care his epistles to the Corinthians, we observe the church believers to be immature. There were divisions, strife and jealousy, but not the practice of sins of death. The proof of this is that only ONE MAN was found committing incest. This case was so unique that in two of his epistles he mentioned it as something unprecedented.

> But actually, I wrote to you not to associate with any so-called brother if he should be an immoral person, or covetous, or an idolater, or a reviler, or a drunkard, or a swindler – not even to eat with such a one.... But those who are outside, God judges. Remove the wicked man from among yourselves.

1 Corinthians 5:11 and 13
(NASB)

In his second epistle he writes to them with a heavy burden for this man:

But if any has caused sorrow, he has caused sorrow not to me, but in some degree – in order not to say too much – to all of you. Sufficient for such a one is this punishment, which was inflicted by the majority.

2 Corinthians 2:5-6

Notice this was not the common denominator of the church. EVERYONE was greatly saddened by just one who had fallen into sin.

Jesus never compromised His principles in order to win souls and have more followers. The rich young man, who approached Him and asks Him how to enter into the kingdom of heaven, was answered with a word that shook him, and made him depart from Jesus sadly.

And, behold, one came and said unto him, Good Master, what good thing shall I do, that I may have eternal life? And he said unto him, Why callest thou me good? There is none good but one, that is, God: but if thou wilt enter into life, keep the commandments. He saith unto him, which? Jesus said, Thou shalt do no murder, Thou shalt not commit adultery, Thou shalt not steal, Thou shalt not bear false witness, Honour thy father and thy mother: and, Thou shalt love thy neighbour as thyself. The young man saith unto him, all these things have I kept from my youth up: what lack I yet? Jesus said unto him, If thou wilt be perfect, go and sell that thou hast, and give to the poor, and thou shalt have treasure in heaven: and come and follow me. But when the young man heard that saying, he went away sorrowful: for he had great possessions.

Matthew 19:16-22

Jesus did not water-down the Gospel to accommodate His greedy soul to make him a convert. Jesus did not speak with the Pharisees in a modern day "evangelistic wisdom", in order to recruit them. Jesus would show them their hearts so they could repent in order to follow him.

Today the young, rich man would be told "Don't worry if you don't want to give up your money (or your lover, your idol, your alcoholism, your hatred, etc.). Jesus loves you and gave His life for you. Allow me to pray a prayer with you, and today, Jesus will come to live in your heart." Really? Do you believe He will come? SELAH.

What are we doing with the Gospel that has the power to save?

The real love, with which God loves us, is a love, with great mercy, showing our condition in order for us to reconcile with the Father. This is the purpose of Jesus Christ, reconciliation. For this to occur, we must understand how much pain our sin causes the Father.

Sin deeply wounds the heart of God, and it deeply wounded Jesus' body and soul. We must not continue preaching a Gospel that avoids confrontation.

7. Called To Be a New Creation in Christ

God desires us to know the depth and meaning of being a new creation in Christ. This is one of the most important foundations of our new life. God is bringing a fresh new illumination on this subject.

This is perhaps one of the most frequently preached topics in the church. However, it is also one of the least understood. So, open your heart because I want you to receive this powerful truth in the light of a new apostolic reformation.

> Therefore if any man be in Christ, he is a new creature: old things are passed away; behold all things are become new.
>
> *2 Corinthians 5:17*

What is Not To Be a New Creation

Being a new creation in Christ does not mean being a member of a church, or changing religion or denomination, or habits, attending a church each day. It does not mean leaving your worldly friends for Christian friends, reading the Bible or enrolling in Christian education courses.

All of these things can be done without ever having become a new creation in Christ. In fact, every religious system using the name of Jesus requires all of these things. Institutions such as the Roman Catholic Church, Jehovah's Witnesses, Mormons, or Masons, require instructions and education in their believe systems.

Religion is the alternative that the devil offers in order to make us believe that we are right with God. Religion makes us believe that the external form of the word is able to supplant the essence of the Spirit.

This alternative is so subtle, it has deceived millions who call themselves Christians. It is for this reason the Spirit uses phrases such as:

> And unto the angel of the church in Sardis write; These things saith he that hath the seven Spirits of God, and the seven stars; I know thy works, that thou hast a name that thou livest, and art dead.

Revelation 3:1

> These are spots in your feasts of charity, when they feast with you, feeding themselves without fear: clouds they are without water, carried about of winds; trees whose fruit withereth, without fruit, twice dead, plucked up by the roots.

Jude 12

The New Creation is the Resurrection of Our Spirit

The new creation is not what we do religiously, but into what we are converted. The conversion is not the adoption of a new philosophy, but a change in the essence of our being.

Something new and wonderful will begin to operate inside of us, which did not exist nor can it be FABRI-CATED. A spiritual creature, different from our soul, born as a result of the resurrection of Christ conceived within our spirit, alive and powerful.

If the flesh is the structure molded by the principles of a fallen nature, the new creation is the spiritual structure molded by the divine nature.

How Does This New Creation Come Into Being?

We must understand the spirit of the natural man is dead as a result of sin. "The wages of sin is death." This means the life of God is not in our spirit. This death is the separation between God and man.

The spirit of the vast majority of human beings is found in a state of lethargy, asleep without the slightest interaction with the soul. In others it has been awakened by spirits of darkness to be used in all forms of occultism, be it New Age, Zen Buddhism, ascetic contemplation, mind control or hallucinogenic drugs. This is why people involved in these practices have spiritual experiences.

In some cases, God Himself awaken the spirit of an individual who does not know Jesus Christ, as in the case of Cornelius, the first Gentile to receive the Gospel. This has happened to the people that have never heard of the Lord. He awakens their spirits in order to reconcile them to Himself.

The spirit is the most powerful part of man, and the devil knows in order to control the spirit world he must activate that region in his followers.

The part of man that is eternal is his spirit. The soul is united with the spirit, accompanying to its final destiny.

The soul is created to interact between the natural world and the spiritual. The soul controlled by the devil after the fall became, the ruler of our being. But the Spirit of man is the essence of each person whether alive or dead asleep or awake.

That is why salvation or condemnation occurs at the level of the spirit. No matter how alive the soul is, no matter how good it may be, its final destiny depends on the condition of the spirit.

A spirit not brought to life with Christ will die. The only thing that can reconcile man with God is Christ. The spirit is where the bridge between God and man is produced. This will not occur at the soul level. The soul does not have life or death (in an eternal sense) in and of itself. It is an instrument helping us to function in the material world.

Man IS A SPIRIT. This is who he is, and is the only place he can receive salvation.

Salvation and the new birth will not occur by an intellectual exercise, but only in the spirit.

The spirit must be impregnated by God.

But as many as received him, to them gave he power to become the sons of God, even to them that believe on his name: which were born, not of blood, nor of the will of the flesh, nor of the will of man, but of God.

John 1:12-13

It is not the will of the flesh, as we have just read, that produces this conception, but God. God's precious seed of life sown in our spirit. This happens when, with a sincere, repentant heart, we surrender to God and are baptized.

Then Peter said unto them, Repent, and be baptized every one of you in the name of Jesus Christ for the remission of sins, and ye shall receive the gift of the Holy Ghost.... Then they that gladly received his word were baptized: and the same day there were added unto them about three thousand souls.

Acts 2:38 and 41

In the New Testament, the true evidence of their faith was demonstrated in their immediate baptism.

He that believeth and is baptized shall be saved...

Mark 16:16

In baptism the Spirit of God and man merge together, so the new spiritual creature can grow into the likeness of God.

The life of God is resurrection life. The power that raised Jesus Christ from the dead now dwells within our spirit.

Baptism is not only entering the water in the name of Jesus. It is the decision to die to our sinful life in order to be reborn in Him. It is crucifying this world with its lusts and passions the same way Jesus did.

Therefore we are buried with him by baptism into death: that like as Christ was raised up from the dead by the glory of the Father, even so we also should walk in newness of life. For if we have been planted together in the likeness of his death, we shall be also in the likeness of his resurrection: knowing this, that our old man is crucified with him, that the body of sin might be destroyed, that henceforth we should not serve sin.

Romans 6:4-6

It is very clear Christ is the model to follow in order to discover the meaning of baptism. I have emphasized words "like as Christ". The model is first death, then resurrection. Baptism is a picture of death. If we do not enter the water with the firm conviction of dying to sin, then, all we have done is get wet. The water itself has no power for salvation. The decision to die is the power to resuscitate. This must be done wholeheartedly and in as much understanding as possible.

People pass through the water, merely fulfilling a religious requirement, without a genuine conviction to follow Jesus Christ with all of their being. Perhaps with a need to be accepted or want to form part of a group in order to feel integrated in society.

I know cases where someone was baptized because he wanted to conquer the heart of a beautiful young lady in the church. Sometimes people are baptized because they feel frustrated with their careers or have failed in business, and want to see if "their luck" changes with this "Christianity" thing.

There are people who join churches because they are lazy, and want the "merciful brothers" to resolve their problems. Others get baptized because someone from the church encouraged them at the last moment on the day baptisms were being performed. I can cite many other situations I have found when ministering to people in the church.

In all of these situations, neither baptism nor conception took place. It is a religious exercise. We are not conceived by "the will of the flesh". This is why we do not see any change or fruit over time in those people in church. They have no idea to evangelize, pray or give tithes or offering.

The new creation is real. It affects our entire being. It invades our mind. It destroys the body of sin. It is the visible light and power of God. It is evangelizing by its very nature, full of life and fire because God Himself is joined to man.

The same way Jesus died and then rose up in resurrection is the model for our new life. When Christ was buried, He was an extremely transformed in the tomb, so much so that He who emerged was totally different from the One who entered. Not even the disciples recognized Him. Paul Himself said, referring to the apostles:

> Wherefore henceforth know we no man after the flesh: yea, though we have known Christ after the flesh, yet now henceforth know we him no more.
>
> *2 Corinthians 5:16*

The new creation is not a manifestation of the flesh, but it is our spirit that is transformed by resurrection.

Once impregnated, the spirit will begin an internal growth. Each part of our spirit is awakened and developed. We perceive a new sensitivity emerging. Things we formerly liked, suddenly we hate. We feel distanced from worldly atmospheres. Hearing vulgar words bothers us. Above all, we hate sinning and grieving the Holy Spirit.

The new creation desires the things from on high. It will not remain silent. It must speak to everyone about Jesus. It enjoys praying and giving. It is brave and loves righteousness. It is filled with fear of God and love towards its neighbor. As the apostle Paul said, it everything as garbage, in order to know Jesus and the power of His resurrection.

Resurrection is not the final state of the sons of God when we are raised from the dead. It is the power that gives life to the new creation that has been conceived inside of us.

> And so it is written, The first man Adam was made a living soul; the last Adam was made a quickening spirit.

> *1 Corinthians 15:45*

If the Spirit of Christ impregnates our spirit, suddenly we are full of life, awakened to a spiritual reality not previously known. Everything within us longs for the things of God. This is not something hypothetical. This new life must have expression and manifestation

However, this is not the experience of all who say, "Lord, Lord!" Iniquity contends the spirits of millions of people in the church. This is why many feel like there are anchors preventing them from making resolute steps towards God. Their eyes are veiled from the Gospel of Jesus Christ will, and they cannot be converted.

They are complacent or resigned to live a religious life. They don't observe in their lives the power of God. Some know very well what is wrong, and others don't have the slightest idea. This might be the most important book that has ever fallen into their hands. It will help them see and identify this terrible scourge that has covered us all and that God wants to remove once and for all from our lives.

In the last chapter of this book, I will explain how to be free from of iniquity and how to truly begin to enjoy the riches of the glory of God that proceed from being impregnated by His Spirit.

4

The Operation and Manifestation of Iniquity

If we could visualize the body of iniquity, it would resemble a twisted black cord in our spirit. It is made from hundreds of thick knots. These knots appear as filthy rags, filled with information and covenants accumulating from generation to generation. It resembles a veil that blocks or hinders the life attempting to move from our spirits to our hearts and eventually to our minds.

Iniquity Produces Spiritual Deafness

Many people have their spiritual hearing obstructed and are unable to hear God's voice.

> The wicked are estranged from the womb: they go astray as soon as they be born, speaking lies. Their poison is like the poison of a serpent: they are like

the deaf adder that stoppeth her ear; which will not hearken to the voice of charmers, charming never so wisely.

Psalm 58:3-5

God's plan is for each of us to hear His voice. This is not just for prophets or for those who have the gift of prophecy. The instructions from the Holy Spirit depend upon our ability to hear God's voice. Entire denominations are closed to this essential truth about the Christian life; professing God no longer speaks today. Nothing is further from the truth. Jesus said, "My sheep hear my voice... and they follow me." (John 10:27) When He said this, the New Testament had not yet been written. He also taught that the Holy Spirit would be sent to teach us all things.

It is written in 1 John:

But ye have an anointing from the Holy One, and ye know all things.

1 John 2:20
(NKJV)

The anointing breaks into our lives and releases revelations from God's word.

The Father designed the spirit of man to be abe to hear His voice. And in fact, every spirit is equipped to hear a variety of voices from the spiritual world. You will agree, every one has heard the devil's voice. We have all heard voices of fear, anxiety, discouragement, negativism, etc. This clearly demonstrates our capacity to hear the spiritual world.

One of the greatest lies from the devil is, we are unable to hear God's voice. What kind of father would God be to have designed his family to hear only the devil's voice?

In fact, if we open our understanding a little, we will realize that God has spoken to us many times. That impulse preventing us from traveling on an airliner for business that ended in a disastrous crash. The sleepless night resulting in our not going to work. Later we discovered brake fluid under our car that would have gone unnoticed had we left for work and could have been devastating. These are examples of God speaking to our spirits that in turn manifest in various parts of our souls.

God's voice is made clear or hindered according to the presence or the absence of iniquity.

> Behold, the LORD'S hand is not shortened, that it cannot save; neither his ear heavy that it cannot hear: but your iniquities have separated between you and your God, and your sins have hid his face from you, that he will not hear.
>
> *Isaiah 59:1-2*

Iniquity can be found in specific areas of our lives." We will explore examples to help clarify some.

Sometimes, a person in ministry may hear clearly what God desires for His church, but may have difficulty concerning financial matters. This could be the result of his past or his ancestors, in which sinful activity in the financial arena occurred. Perhaps fraudulent business was conducted harming innocent persons. As long as this is not confessed as sin and iniquity, it will create blockage in the spiritual ear, as well as attract problems in finances.

It is extremely important to make a detailed analysis of our works and those of our ancestors in order to identify our iniquity. Of course, this is impossible without the revelation of the Holy Spirit.

We must tell Him that we want to eliminate all iniquity from our being, asking Him to show us where iniquity is rooted in our lives.

Sometimes our spiritual ear is obstructed and we need the help of a minister of God to assist us in the areas of iniquity. It is easy to fall into spiritual laziness and carelessness. "Letting others hear for us, because we don't hear anything!" This is iniquity in action.

This also happens in other areas of our soul, such as our emotions. People who are unable to hear God's voice can be consumed with sexual dreams and aberrations. They pray, asking forgiveness for their dreams or their fantasies, but never seem to be free. The reason is, unconfessed iniquity.

The vast majority of people make general confessions, such as, "Lord, forgive all sexual sin that I or my ancestors have committed." Unfortunately this does not help much. It might be enough in the case of a deathbed confession, but it is not enough for the rest of us.

In the spiritual world, every sin grows from the root of iniquity. It is very important to make a detailed list, assisted by the Holy Spirit, and ask forgiveness for each of our actions.

There are people who fill an entire notebook, recording one by one all of their sins. If you will take the time to do this, you will be totally free and live a life of peace. This is important for married couples, whose lives are riddled with guilt from sexual dreams and fantasies, frequently undermining their sex life.

Dear reader, God has not abandoned you, but iniquity is a greater hindrance than you realize.

Iniquity Produces Spiritual Blindness

The same way God designed us to have spiritual hearing, He planned we would have spiritual eyes. These are the eyes of understanding, which permits us to see with clarity God's truths and glorious treasure of His riches. Our spiritual eyes allow us to see the invisible world and be transformed from glory to glory.

Can anyone see into the spiritual world? Of course they can. But in order to operate from the truth we must understand how it applies to our lives.

Before our personal encounter with Christ, we did not know we could heal the sick or cast out demons. Perhaps, we were taught that these things are not for today.

In my case, when I read in the Word: "These signs would follow those who believed in Jesus", I fully believed, and the Word became alive. The same thing happened when I realized we could see the kingdom of God and this was not just for a few people, but also for everyone who was converted with all their heart.

> Nevertheless when it shall turn to the Lord, the veil shall be taken away. Now the Lord is that Spirit: and where the Spirit of the Lord is, there is liberty. But WE ALL, with open face beholding as in a glass the

glory of the Lord, are changed into the same image from glory to glory, even as by the Spirit of the Lord.

2 Corinthians 3:16-18

Clearly when the Spirit of God is present; He permits us to see His glory.

This is a reality that thousands of people are living. The question is why can't all people see it? In most cases, there are two reasons. The first is veils of iniquity have not been understood or removed from their spiritual senses. Secondly, for those mature in the Lord, have not developed their spiritual vision, or have never believed it was possible or simply not thought it was important. Others may not have recognized it as necessary, in comparison to other gifts.

But let's focus on the first cause, the veils of iniquity.

The apostle Paul points out the work of the devil focused on producing spiritual blindness.

In whom the god of this world hath blinded the minds of them which believe not, lest the light of the glorious gospel of Christ, who is the image of God, should shine unto them.

2 Corinthians 4:4

He also says:

In fact, their minds were grown hard and calloused – they had become dull and had lost the power of understanding; for until this present day, when the Old Testament [the old covenant] is being read, that same veil still lies [on their hearts], not being lifted [to reveal] that in Christ it is made void and done away. Yes, down to this [very] day whenever Moses is read a veil lies upon their minds and hearts. But whenever a person turns (in repentance) to the Lord the veil is stripped off and taken away.

2 Corinthians 3:14-16
(Amplified Bible)

Now, even though the apostle undeniably is referring to those who have never approached Christ, he is also speaking of those in whom there is unbelief. Thousands of Christians have believed in Jesus as their Savior, but in many areas of their lives they are unbelievers.

The reason is, their hearts are still contaminated with iniquity and have not been purged. This formed veils of varying intensities producing spiritual blindness. In order to remove them, it is necessary to identify the areas of our heart that have not yet been surrendered to the lordship of Christ. When these areas are converted the veils will be removed.

Only the presence of the Holy Spirit can transform our hearts. He is the One who sets the captives free from prisons of the heart and mind that have been in darkness. That is why it is important to spend time with the Lord, in the measure necessary for His glory to change our lives. Then we will see the light that can transform us into His image.

Christ is the image of the invisible God, and it is His image in us that beholds with open face the glory of God. Jesus said:

Yet a little while, and the world seeth me no more; but YE SEE ME.

John 14:19a

He also taught, saying:

As thou hast sent me into the world, even so have I also sent them into the world.

John 17:18

Jesus was sent, full of the Holy Spirit and the ability to see and hear everything the Father was doing. Likewise, He sends us, seeing and hearing what He does.

Then answered Jesus and said unto them, Verily, verily, I say unto you, The Son can do nothing of himself, but what he seeth the Father do.... For the Father loveth the Son, and showeth him all things that himself doeth....

John 5:19a-20a

The majority of God's children do not move in this liberty, because iniquity fills them with unbelief or guilt. This is nothing more than veils of darkness with which the devil have blinded the Church. His objective is a Church powerless to move in the fullness Jesus has bought with His blood.

Seeing the kingdom of God and beholding His glory is the most wonderful thing that could happen to us. It is worth doing whatever necessary to obtain it. The price is to cleanse our hearts of iniquity.

Iniquity Produces Sickness and Pain

Iniquity is the principle cause of sickness. Although its origin is in the spirit of man, it travels through the soul and results as a physical manifestation destroying the body.

Science recognizes something called psychosomatic illnesses. According to the doctors, this type of disease originates in the mind, and produces chemical reactions in the organism. This is in a large part a response of our body to feelings of hatred, bitterness, resentment, shame, etc.

The reality is this problem is much deeper than a mere chemical reaction. It is a spiritual matter. It results from iniquity that is carried from generation to generation. It is so deep that it will affect the genetics of our physical bodies.

This iniquity with which we are born, intensifies as we contaminate our hearts with sin.

We have observed, the spirit, soul and body intimately intertwine. The condition of the first two will determine the condition of the entire organism.

The apostle John says in his third epistle:

Beloved, I wish above all things that thou mayest prosper and be in health, even as thy soul prospereth.

3 John 1:2

A spirit, filled with the presence of God along with a pure heart, having been purged of iniquity, will result in a healthy body; the opposite will be true for those in which iniquity has gone unchecked.

As he clothed himself with cursing like as with his garment, so let it come into his bowels like water, and like oil into his bones.

Psalm 109:18

This psalm speaks about a wicked man or one who has iniquity. Iniquity forms a type of toxic liquid, which accumulates in organs, deteriorating ones general state of health.

Iniquity also resides in the bones, weakening them along with the blood. Life is found in the blood, according to the Bible, and it is in the bone marrow where blood is produced. All illnesses in the blood originates from iniquity, such as diabetes, leukemia, high or low blood pressure, lupus, etc.

Sadness, if not from the Lord will produce death (2 Corinthians 7:10b). Death clings to iniquity and penetrates the bones.

Have mercy upon me, O LORD, for I am in trouble: mine eye is consumed with grief, yea, my soul and my belly. For my life is spent with grief, and my years with sighing: my strength faileth because of mine INIQUITY, and my bones are consumed.

Psalm 31:9-10

Sickness residing in the bones and joints, such as osteoporosis, arthritis and rheumatic pain are the result of continual impregnation of secretion originating from iniquity.

The formation of tumors and sharp muscular pain can be the result of the physical body's reaction to this spiritual inheritance.

None calleth for justice, nor any pleadeth for truth: they trust in vanity, and speak lies; they conceive mischief, and bring forth iniquity. They hatch cockatrice' eggs, and weave the spider's web: he that eateth of their eggs dieth, and that which is crushed breaketh out into a viper Isaiah 59:4-5

Many times the Lord shows us the way iniquity penetrates the body in the shape of eggs. These eggs form tumors or cancers, which then, spread and multiply throughout other organs.

Iniquity and the Captivity of the Soul

Iniquity manifests in the body as black water and make the body sick. However, the origin of these substances is from the spirit of man.

Iniquity inside of the human being will affect his whole environment. It is like a fountain that flows from his inner being, made of muddy waters contaminating everything it touches. These waters create spiritual swamps in which the soul gets stuck. Righteous people even sin without, any reason or understanding as if trapped in a murky pit.

Let's look at this in the Word:

But the wicked are like the troubled sea, when it cannot rest, whose waters cast up mire and dirt.

Isaiah 57:20

Notice in this next verse how the righteous are trapped by collective iniquity:

...For our transgressions are with us; and as for our iniquities, we know them; in transgressing and lying against the LORD, and departing away from our God, speaking oppression and revolt, conceiving and uttering from the heart words of falsehood. And judgment is turned away backward, and justice standeth afar off: for truth is fallen in the street, and equity cannot enter. Yea, truth faileth; and he that departeth from evil maketh himself a prey: and the LORD saw it, and it displeased him that there was no judgment.

Isaiah 59:12b-15

Spiritually this mud of iniquity is cast upon others through violent perverse words, threats, slander, unjust accusations and pressures. People with this mud have controlling spirits, which oppress, castrate, and manipulate, polluting the places where they reside.

Psychological problems, such as claustrophobia, originate from this type of spiritual environment. Many times, even though the conditions have changed, the soul remains captive in the past, and deliverance becomes necessary.

Surrounded by these waters may generate fear, nightmares, and great desperation. King David many times found himself surrounded by these muddy waters that literally were drowning him.

Because of the VOICE OF THE ENEMY, because of the oppression of the wicked: for THEY CAST INIQUITY UPON ME, and in wrath they hate me. My heart is sore pained within me: and the terrors of death are fallen upon me. Fearfulness and trembling are come upon me, and horror hath overwhelmed me.

Psalm 55:3-5

Save me, O God; for the waters are come in unto my soul. I sink in deep mire, where there is no standing: I am come into deep waters, where the floods overflow me. I am weary of my crying: my throat is dried: mine eyes fail while I wait for my God. They that hate me without a cause are more than the hairs of mine head: they that would destroy me, being mine enemies wrongfully, are mighty: then I restored that which I took not away.

Psalm 69:1-4

This mud is real in the spiritual world; it feels as though one was in quick sand and only through the power of God is one able to escape. These situations are frustrating because there appear to be no way out. Nothing to hold, and the more we struggle the more we sink.

We find this condition in the soul of the psalmist who has been harassed by evil. Iniquity has been cast upon him, and his soul has entered into captivity:

For my soul is full of troubles: and my life draweth nigh unto the grave.... Thou hast laid me in the lowest pit, in darkness, in the deeps.... I am shut up, and I cannot come forth.

Psalm 88: 3, 6, and 8b

When we see the spiritual world, we see this quick sand as a place the devil has imprisoned a part of the soul, releasing oppression and calamity.

The soul is fragmented and held captive as a result of iniquity, traumas or evil harassment.

King David cries out to God in situations like this in which he is terribly oppressed by the iniquity of his enemies:

> The sorrows of death compassed me, and the floods of ungodly men made me afraid. The sorrows of hell compassed me about: the snares of death prevented me.

Psalm 18:4-5

He also says:

> For without cause have they hid for me their net in a pit, which without cause they have digged for my soul.

Psalm 35:7

Job also speaks of these holes:

> Yea, ye overwhelm the fatherless, and ye dig a pit for your friend.

Job 6:27

People that cast iniquity, hatred and curses do not only produce these prisons of darkness, but our own choices trap us in places of great affliction.

Such as sit in darkness and in the shadow of death, being bound in affliction and iron; because they rebelled against the words of God, and contemned the counsel of the most High.... Fools because of their transgression, and because of their iniquities, are afflicted. Their soul abhorreth all manner of meat; and they draw near unto the gates of death.

Psalm 107:10-11 and 17-18

Those who do not give the glory to God are also trapped in these places:

Hear ye, and give ear; be not proud: for the LORD hath spoken. Give glory to the LORD your God, before he cause darkness, and before your feet stumble upon the dark mountains, and, while ye look for light, he turn it into the shadow of death, and make it gross darkness. But if ye will not hear it, my soul shall weep in secret places for your pride; and mine eye shall weep sore, and run down with tears, because the Lord's flock is carried away captive.

Jeremiah 13:15-17

Direction must originate from the Holy Spirit if we are to rescue souls from these pits. We must have permission from God to remove persons from these places. We must ask Him to show us by the Spirit the cause of captivity in the first place. The Lord will show us through the gifts of the Spirit how such situations occurred. Then we must ask forgiveness for our sin, iniquity, or rebellion. We must forgive those who have done us harm, and finally, command the captive soul to "BE SET FREE." For those who dwell in regions of darkness we must tell them, "To LEAVE THE DARKNESS AND COME INTO THE LIGHT."

> Thus saith the LORD, In an acceptable time have I heard thee, and in a day of salvation have I helped thee: and I will preserve thee, and give thee for a covenant of the people, to establish the earth, to cause to inherit the desolate heritages; that thou mayest say to the prisoners, Go forth; to them that are in darkness, Show yourselves. They shall feed in the ways, and their pastures shall be in all high places.
>
> *Isaiah 49:8-9*

There are times when we must take them by the hand and remove them from the hole. Spiritually, the deliverer as well as the one being set free may experience a sensation of victory and liberty. Then, we ask God to place this soul in heavenly places, in order to be nurtured by the Holy Spirit. The results of a deliverance of this kind are beyond description.

Iniquity Produces Financial Ruin and Lack

Iniquity began in Lucifer, originating in the twisted thought that penetrated his heart, making him believe he could be equal to God. The origin was because of the abundance of his riches. In Ezekiel chapters 27 and 28, the Bible describes the power of his commercial dealings and refers to him as the King of Tyre, the capital of commerce at that time.

The fall of Lucifer is intimately tied to commerce and riches. It is from this love for riches that Babylon emerges, the spiritual city from where he governs the kingdoms of the world.

> So he carried me away in the spirit into the wilderness: and I saw a woman sit upon a scarlet coloured beast, full of names of blasphemy, having seven heads and ten horns. And the woman was arrayed in purple and scarlet colour, and decked with gold and precious stones and pearls, having a golden cup in her hand full of abominations and filthiness of her fornication: And upon her forehead was a name written, MYSTERY, BABYLON THE GREAT, THE MOTHER OF HARLOTS AND ABOMINATIONS OF THE EARTH.... And the woman which thou sawest is that great city, which reigneth over the kings of the earth.

> *Revelation 17:3-5 and 18*

There is a part of commerce and riches that is righteous and necessary for the people of the earth. But in a very subtle manner, iniquity, the devil's seed, used this fertile soil to sow his twisted evil nature.

All nations have participated in its seduction, and therefore, are trapped in its nets.

> For all nations have drunk of the wine of the wrath of her fornication, and the kings of the earth have committed fornication with her, and the merchants of the earth are waxed rich through the abundance of her delicacies. And I heard another voice from heaven,

saying, Come out of her, my people, that ye be not partakers of her sins, and that ye receive not of her plagues.

Revelation 18:3-4

Commerce and riches have brightness, which becomes the door iniquity, enters. This splendor is a glory that does not come from God. A feeling of security and power artificially rises up, taking the place of God. The brilliance charms and seduces the world.

The riches created in Lucifer's heart a narcosis, making him believe the power of his wealth made him equal to the Most High.

By the multitude of thy merchandise they have filled the midst of thee with violence, and thou hast sinned: therefore I will cast thee as profane out of the mountain of God: and I will destroy thee, O covering cherub, from the midst of the stones of fire. Thine heart was lifted up because of thy beauty, thou hast corrupted thy wisdom by reason of thy brightness: I will cast thee to the ground, I will lay thee before kings, that they may behold thee.

Ezekiel 28:16-17

Iniquity, formed in the heart of Lucifer because of the beauty and splendor of his treasures. Everything was distorted in him; to the degree His creator God, became less important than the gold, and precious stones. This distortion is the same satanic seed planted in the heart of men at birth.

From the beginning of time, man because of iniquity has searched more for gold than for God. Commerce is impregnated with iniquity in all possible forms. To some degree, this heritage is in the bloodline of nearly all men.

The love of possessions, create in people all types of evil. Throughout the centuries, gold has been stained with blood once and again. The one, who owns the most, wields power! This is the slogan of every western civilization.

In almost every pagan culture, gold has been revered in order to be offered to their gods. It has been the symbol of power in European kingdoms. The most abominable crime organizations are the result of the love for riches.

Millions of Christians spend more time in the pursuit of riches than the pursuit of God. When people are consumed with the goods and comforts of this world, the churches reflect this iniquity; forgetting the poor, homeless and widows. We are full of iniquity when it has become more of a priority to sacrifice and struggle in order to obtain something of this world than it is to sacrifice our lives in order to find higher levels with God.

When our possessions, salary, or businesses become our security and not God, we have fallen into the same business dealings that destroyed Lucifer.

The economy of the world is full of iniquity and blood shedding. War is waged over money. Arms are sold to terrorists. Entire nations are allowed to die of hunger in order to maintain market price. Banking systems are corrupt; governments sell their integrity for money. Justice is corrupted with gold; one can silence justice even in homicide and pursue the defenseless. Fraud is conducted with citizens' money, in a system filled with filth, fornication, robbery, lies and deceit. I don't believe I err when I say most sins have money as a common denominator.

The devil weaves powerful blindfolds in order to justify all types of sin in the financial arena. God is robbed at every turn in tithes and offerings. He who is in lack justifies cheating and lying to his brother. It is easy for a person to borrow money from someone and not repay the debt, because money is more important than friendship.

On the subject of finances is where I have observed the least fear of God. People are unaware that consuming oneself with money and becoming its servant is signing a covenant with death.

Notice how iniquity-surrounding riches is intimately tied to spirits of death.

> I will incline mine ear to a parable: I will open my dark saying upon the harp. Wherefore should I fear in the days of evil, when the iniquity of my heels shall compass me about. This is their way is their folly: yet their posterity approve their sayings. Selah. Like sheep they are laid in the grave; death shall feed on them; and the upright shall have dominion over them in the morning; and their beauty shall consume in the grave from their dwelling. But God will redeem my soul from the power of the grave: for he shall receive me. Selah.

> *Psalm 49:5-6 and 13-15*

Sheol, is the place of the dead. However, in this psalm this place exercises an influence and power over those who are alive. The same way, in which heaven exercises power over the just and the unjust, death also captivates and guides those in iniquity, rebellion, and sin.

Money should only be an instrument in our hands, not a source of security that many had made it. God has begun to judge the Babylonian system, which is this financial structure

Rev 18

Because ye have said, we have made a covenant with death and with hell are we at agreement; when the overflowing scourge shall pass through, it shall not come unto us: for we have made lies our refuge, and under falsehood have we hid ourselves: Therefore, thus saith the Lord God, Behold I lay in Zion for a foundation a stone, a tried stone, a precious stone, a sure foundation: he hath believeth shall not make haste.

Judgment also will I lay to the line, and righteousness to the plummet: and the hail shall sweep away the refuge of lies, and the waters shall overflow the hiding place.

Isaiah 28:15-17

Trusts in riches are not a privilege of only the wealthy. Anyone who has his trust or faith in anything other than God is serving mammon.

Financial iniquity attracts to itself judgments of ruin.

Therefore, I will judge you oh house of Israel, everyone according to his ways, saith the Lord God.

Repent, and turn yourselves from all your transgressions; so iniquity shall not be your ruin.

Ezekiel 18:30

Both of my grandparents were very wealthy. Nevertheless, their lives ended in financial ruin. When I became a Christian I had very little money and each time I received a blessing from the Lord, it was immediately stolen by the devil. Even my parent's inheritance was taken from me unrighteously.

I didn't understand why I was losing my financial inheritance until I began to understand iniquity. One day I asked the Lord to show me the financial iniquity in my lineage. I had a dream in which I saw one of my grandparents committing fraud with one of his business associates. This man cursed him and all of his generations were affected with financial ruins.

The next morning, the first thing I did was to ask forgiveness for the iniquity and sin of my grandfather and to cancel any curse, placing the sacrifice of Christ between my grandfather and his descendents. Then, I began to search out the areas in which I had sinned by placing my confidence in riches or any other sin in the area of money that I could have committed. I asked for forgiveness. From that day forward, God has returned to me everything the devil had stolen and the blessings of Jehovah rest upon my life.

It was riches and commercial dealings, which produced pride and eventually the fall of Lucifer. This is why it is important to analyze the origin and motive of each commercial transaction to detect any connection with iniquity that will sooner or later bring ruin.

For example, many businesses have been consecrated to idols. Other people may purchase a business unfairly resulting in abuses to the former owner. Businesses may have been created with unclean money a partnership with an unscrupulous person, will affect the business because of sins. There are illegal business transactions conducted with merchants who abuse their employees. Bribery, if used in obtaining of permits will cause problems. Sometimes, one can sell an unworthy product or can advertise one level of quality and deliver something less. Each case is diverse, but each is worthy of examination.

Many people think God wants to bless them financially, regardless of the means. I have witnessed many ungodly transactions done to unbelievers by those calling themselves Christians, shielding themselves behind Proverbs 13:22, where it says the money of the sinners will pass to the hands of the righteous.

Today, many marketing methods are filled with lies and deceit, in order to trap the client. God takes all of this very seriously, and it prevents Him from hearing our prayers.

> Behold, the LORD'S hand is not shortened, that it cannot save; neither his ear heavy that it cannot hear: but your iniquities have separated between you and your God, and your sins have hid his face from you, that he will not hear. For your hands are defiled with blood, and your fingers with iniquity (the works of your hands); your lips have spoken lies, your tongue hath muttered perverseness. None calleth for justice,

nor any pleadeth for truth: they trust in vanity, and speak lies; they conceive mischief, and bring forth iniquity.

Isaiah 59:1-4

In order to be free from this situation, we must confess our sins and iniquity, and in the situation where we have offended someone, it is necessary to restore in whatever ways is possible. There are cases where this is impossible. If we are involved in wrongdoing, we must cease immediately. If we don't, sooner or later, ruin will visit us and our descendents.

Iniquity and Grievance

Grievance is an injustice done to someone in whom this person remains in grief and dishonor. It is an attack of injustice that affects the very core of a person's being. It is marked by an offence that destroys essential parts of the "heart." It is an impartation of iniquity into the inner most being.

The presence of this grievance in a person acts as a powerful magnet, attracting offences and injustices. One way iniquity manifests itself is through the tongue, as slander and gossip. Our tongue determines many of the curses or blessings we receive.

Death and life are in the power of the tongue: and they that love it shall eat the fruit thereof.

Proverbs 18:21

The tongue expresses what is in the heart, as illustrated by the apostle Luke:

...For of the abundance of the heart his mouth speaketh.

Luke 6:45b

A heart weighed down with iniquity continually talks negatively about other people. They are not careful in how they express themselves, either through profanity or cursing. They create division and offend others as if they had daggers in their mouths. These people are negative. This is the result of multiple offences and injustices that continually plague them. This type of iniquity produces a vicious cycle of destroying and being destroyed.

People, who have been rejected, appear to attract more and more rejection. Partly because they are trapped in nets of iniquity, and because of a spiritual law in operation. This law will continue until iniquity is removed from their lineage.

People who have been abused in some way, either incestuously or psychological, become victims of injustice. As if they wear a bull's-eye on their back.

In the case of incest (sexual relations with a family member), iniquity is so strong that it attracts many kinds of curses, such as those described in Deuteronomy 28. The abused person must forgive and ask for forgiveness for the sins of his ancestors. Many similar cases exist in the family lineages, which were the very root cause that influenced the father or family member to commit this aberration.

Have the workers of iniquity no knowledge? Who eat up my people as they eat bread: they have not called upon God.

Psalm 53:4

In order to stop this cycle of injustice and grievance, one must search his or her heart, identifying occasions in which the injustice occurred. Then, if you do not know the instance where this sin and iniquity originated ask for revelation. Ask God's forgiveness for the iniquity of your ancestors in this area.

When your tongue has slandered and abused someone, causing pain and inflicting deep wounds, it is necessary to bring restitution. Repent before God. This is the first step, but this will not remove the seed of iniquity you have sown against yourself. Ask forgiveness form those you have harmed. You must do something good for them to attempt to undo the evil that you have caused.

Wash you, make you clean; put away the evil of your doings from before mine eyes; cease to do evil; learn to do well; seek judgment, relieve the oppressed, judge the fatherless, plead for the widow.

Isaiah 1:16-17

Iniquity and the Spirit of Fornication

Idol worship is a work of iniquity that God hates. In Latin America, gods are made in sculpted form. In Europe and in North America, these gods are money, comfort and culture, although images are also worshipped.

Unfortunately, idolatry is the beginning of a series of sins, directed by the spirit of fornication.

Today, nations are overrun with bold licentiousness and sexual depravation. Even in the Church, as a result of the lack or no fear of God, sins of adultery, pornography and fornication are proliferating.

My heart is troubled, because I see Churches knowledgeable in the Word, anointing, prophecy and other gifts of God. Yet, Christians seem to be so hardened, nothing makes them change. Of course, there are beautiful people in Christ, holy and fearful of God. But the majority remains fearless, because the nations are full of idolatrous iniquity.

In the majority of cases, the people, at least in Latin America, have left wooden idols, but remain trapped by this spirit of fornication preventing them from knowing God fully.

Whoredom and wine and new wine take away the heart. My people ask counsel at their stocks, and their staff declareth unto them: for the spirit of whoredoms hath caused them to err, and they have gone a whoring from under their God. They sacrifice upon the tops of the mountains, and burn incense upon the hills, under oaks and poplars and elms, because the shadow thereof is good: therefore your daughters shall commit whoredom, and your spouses shall commit adultery. I will not punish your daughters when they commit whoredom, nor your spouses when they commit adultery: for themselves are separated with whores, and they sacrifice with harlots: therefore the people that doth not understand shall fall.... They will not frame their doings to turn unto their God: for the spirit of whoredoms is in the midst of them, and they have not known the LORD.

Hosea 4:11-14 and 5:4

Where there is or has been idolatry, the spirit of fornication is loosed. It is important to uproot iniquity in depth and precision. General repentance is superficial, but the root and the essence of the problem is left untreated. Sooner or later sexual sins will manifest.

Fornication is not only physical, but also a condition of the heart infected with iniquity. This hinders people from knowing God intimately and embracing Him wholeheartedly. It manifests in people who want pleasant experiences with the Holy Spirit. They desire the warmth of a relationship, but not the commitment of a marriage with God.

This type of iniquity causes people to be pursued continually by sexual dreams, vile and obscene thoughts. I have known people desperate to escape this situation, but have no idea what to do in order to be free.

The solution is to take a pencil and paper, and write a detailed list of idols adored by themselves or family members. You must make a note of the pacts made with such images or spirits, and promises or gifts made. Ask God to forgive you and your ancestors for this iniquity and command it to be uprooted from your lives.

In addition, you must identify all situations in which you had sexual interaction outside of marriage, such as fornication, pornography, masturbation, incest, adultery, etc. It is important to be specific. If a person has had a promiscuous life, it may be difficult to remember all of the names. However, all of this information is registered in our spirit and the Holy Spirit is able to remind us of each instance. Perhaps he will do it all at once, or it may take weeks. That's fine. The important thing is that we do it and then, we will enjoy a beautiful liberty and powerful intimacy with our beloved Lord.

Once this is completed, it is important to declare the freedom form our descendents.

Iniquity and Cities of Desolation

Iniquity not only affects the life of an individual, but the destruction of cities are the result of this invisible assassin.

Since the fall of man, iniquity has become part of his being; the earth absorbed this seed of evil, and became cursed.

And unto Adam he said, Because thou hast hearkened unto the voice of thy wife, and hast eaten of the tree, of which I commanded thee, saying, Thou shalt not eat of it: cursed is the ground for thy sake; in sorrow shalt thou eat of it all the days of thy life.

Genesis 3:17

From that point creation has groaned to see the glorious manifestation of the sons of God. The Lord has given man the earth, and although we lost the lordship of it, it is still our responsibility to declare its redemption through the sacrifice of Jesus. If it is true that we have been a curse for the earth, the opposite is also true. We can be a blessing and eat from it in joy and peace.

Iniquity penetrated the earth the moment of the fall, but our iniquity continues the contamination...

Do ye indeed speak righteousness, O congregation? Do ye judge uprightly, O ye sons of men? Yea, in heart ye work wickedness; ye weigh the violence of your hands in the earth.

Psalm 58:1-2

Entire cities are founded through territorial consecrations to pagan gods, Masonic designs, magic geometry, horrendous sacrifices and blood shedding. All of this has repercussions, making it necessary to redeem the city.

Woe to him that buildeth a town with blood, and stablisheth a city by iniquity!

Habakkuk 2:12

The same way, in which iniquity digs holes to trap souls of individuals, entire cities remain trapped in darkness, violence, and corruption.

The nations have sunk down in the pit that they made: in the net which they hid is their own foot caught.

Psalm 9:15
(Amplified Bible)

It is important for the righteous to pray and work to bring healing to the cities.

If they shall confess their iniquity, and the iniquity of their fathers, with their trespass which they trespassed against me, and that also they have walked contrary unto me; and that I also have walked contrary unto them, and have brought them into the land of their enemies; if then their uncircumcised hearts be humbled, and they then accept of the punishment of their iniquity: Then will I remember my covenant with Jacob, and also my covenant with Isaac, and also my covenant with Abraham will I remember; and I WILL REMEMBER THE LAND.

Leviticus 26:40-42

Iniquity and Curses

Blessings as well as curses are spiritual laws, searching for places which to attach themselves like a bird in flight, looking for a place to nest in order to establish and fulfill its purpose.

As the bird by wandering, as the swallow by flying, so the curse causeless shall not come.

Proverbs 26:2

At the same time, we see in Deuteronomy chapter 28:

And all these blessings shall come on thee, and OVERTAKE THEE, if thou shalt hearken unto the voice of the LORD thy God.... But it shall come to pass, if thou wilt not hearken unto the voice of the LORD thy God, to observe to do all his commandments and his statutes which I command thee this

day; that all these curses shall come upon thee, and
OVERTAKE THEE.

Deuteronomy 28:2 and 15

X Many times I find people who, after having read books
or hearing teachings about curses, revoke them and cancel
them in their lives, but over time they return. The reason
is the power of the Spirit succeeded in removing them for
a time, but their cause was never uprooted, which was
iniquity.

If we imagine the form of iniquity, it would look like a
twisted, black cord inside of us. It is made with of hundreds
of knots and layer upon layer, making it thick. These layers
are like filthy rags, full of information and covenants that
have been accumulating from generation to generation.
Large quantities of curses cling to this cord, as well as
decrees we make along with our ancestors.

The sin of Judah is written with a pen of iron, and
with the point of a diamond: it is graven upon the
table of their heart, and upon the horns of your altars.

Jeremiah 17:1

This body of iniquity records all the sins committed
by prior generations. It is precisely from this information
that sin grows and manifests itself. This information is not
removed through a general prayer, such as, "Lord, erase all
my iniquities." Sin, rebellion and iniquity require observa-
tion and analysis of our heart.

At the time of a genuine conversion Jesus takes our
repentant heart to give us salvation, even though we have

not confessed all of our sins. However, from that point, the Holy Spirit begins to reform our conscience, illuminating our understanding about sins we never even knew to be transgression. He will cause us to repent of these things in our lives of which we were previously ignorant. If we surrender to the Lord, He will lead us to repent in each area needed for our sanctification.

He deals with our iniquities in the same way, since it is here the root of our problem is found and more demonic activity is woven.

> Blessed is the man unto whom the LORD imputeth not iniquity, and in whose spirit there is no guile. When I kept silence, my bones waxed old through my roaring all the day long. For day and night thy hand was heavy upon me: my moisture is turned into the drought of summer. Selah. I acknowledged my sin unto thee, and MINE INIQUITY HAVE I NOT HID. I said, I will confess my transgressions unto the LORD; and thou forgavest THE INIQUITY OF MY SIN. Selah.

> *Psalm 32:2-5*

The redemptive work of God goes to the very depths of the matter, to the very place where sin originated. If we only deal with sin in a superficial manner, the body of iniquity will continue to thrive.

To study iniquity in relation to curses, make it necessary to identify through prayer the root of iniquity that produced such curses, and then uprooting them one at a time.

What is a curse?

I like the definition given by the apostle John Eckhard in his book Identifying and Removing Curses: "A curse is the penalty given by God to a person and to his descendents as the result of their iniquity."

> Render unto them recompense, O LORD, according to the work of their hands. Give them sorrow of heart, thy curse unto them.

Lamentations 3:64-65

Curses can be identified through various recurring symptoms, which spring from specific roots of iniquity:

- Chronic financial problems, poverty and misery, land that does not produce fruit, business that dry up for no apparent reason.

  Cause: Robbery, fraud, witchcraft, idolatry, trusting in man before God, robbing God of tithes and offerings (Malachi 3:8-9), swearing falsely in the name of God (Zechariah 5:4).

- Gynecologic problems in the woman: continual flow of blood, chronic menstrual disorders, sterility and miscarriage.

  Cause: Incest, adultery, divorce, sexual perversion, abortion, pornography, fornication, sexual abuse, rebellion and disobedience (Genesis 3:16).

- Chronic or diverse illnesses, one after another.

  Cause: Idolatry, witchcraft, blood shedding (Deuteronomy 28:27 and 35).

- Fungus problems on the skin or nails, fevers and causalities.

  Cause: Witchcraft, unclean practices, curses cast upon a person (Deuteronomy 28:22).

- Accident Prone.

  Cause: Homicide, death, blood shedding, death cult, spiritualism, witchcraft, idolatry and Satanism (Deuteronomy 28).

- Marital problems, divorce and disloyal spouse.

  Cause: Divorce, disloyalty, idolatry, witchcraft, incest and adultery (Deuteronomy 28:30).

- Premature death and suicide.

  Cause: Homicide, blood shedding, idolatry, witch-craft and the love of money (Proverbs 2:22, Psalm 37:28).

- Problems of continual robbery, fraud, frozen inheri-tances, loss of houses or properties.

  Cause: Robbery, fraud, illegal traffic of merchandise, slave trade or white slave trade (Zechariah 5:3-4).

- Mental problems, insanity, Alzheimer's and senile dementia.

  Cause: Pride, haughtiness, trusting in riches and stubbornness (Daniel 4:32, Deuteronomy 28:18).

- Destruction of different types.

    Cause: Homicide, violence, drunkenness, drug addiction, witchcraft, idolatry and suicide (Deuteronomy 28:20).

- Grievances and abuse of all kinds.

    Cause: Rape, abuse, slander and a slanderous tongue (Psalm 53:4).

- Becoming a wanderer or a vagabond, being thrown out of one's own country, living as illegal in a foreign land.

    Cause: Homicide and trusting in riches (Genesis 4:12 and Psalm 109:10). Sexual sin and disobedience to God.

- Defeat before one's enemies.

    Cause: Idolatry, witchcraft and rebellion (Deuteronomy 28:25).

When someone detects that he is under a curse, the first thing they must do is determine the cause. This can be found in oneself or in one's lineage. Usually it is found in both. Sometimes we need the Holy Spirit to reveal things of the past, as in the case I related about my grandfather.

Next, you must repent of iniquity, and then uproot it from your spirit by the means of a declaration. Once this is done, you must revoke and cancel the curses, breaking their power over your life. To conclude, proclaim upon your life the victory where He was made a curse to set us free.

Christ hath redeemed us from the curse of the law, being made a curse for us: for it is written, Cursed is every one that hangeth on a tree: that the blessing of Abraham might come on the Gentiles through Jesus Christ; that we might receive the promise of the Spirit through faith.

Galatians 3:13-14

5

The Power of Attraction
of Spiritual Forces

Righteousness and iniquity are spiritual forces, creating a tremendous force of attraction. The first one is intrinsically tied to the throne of God, and the other, to the devil's. Righteousness is an attribute of the Lord that lines everything up with the kingdom of God. Iniquity is the opposite force that twists and perverts everything, separating it from the designs of God.

Jesus, desiring to teach us a powerful truth, tells us in His Word:

> Therefore I say unto you, Take no thought for your life, what ye shall eat, or what ye shall drink; nor yet for your body, what ye shall put on. Is not the life more than meat, and the body than raiment? Therefore take no thought, saying, What shall we eat? Or,

what shall we drink? Or, Wherewithal shall we be clothed? (For after all these things do the Gentiles seek :) for your heavenly Father knoweth that ye have need of all these things. But seek ye first the kingdom of God, and his righteousness; and all these things shall be added unto you.

Matthew 6:25 and 31-33

If we approach the kingdom of God and His righteousness a power of attraction is produced drawing all things of His Kingdom towards us.

The righteousness of God contains within itself a powerful force that continually judges iniquity, fighting with it in order to bring things in line with God. On the other hand, this force also pulls everything that has to do with the kingdom of heaven. It attracts blessing from on high. It pulls towards itself all spiritual and material riches. This is because righteousness is intimately tied to the glory of God. They go hand in hand, manifesting themselves simultaneously.

The heavens declare his righteousness, and all the people see his glory.

Psalm 97:6

Isaiah talks about this magnetic power and it's manifestation in the believer who is established in the righteousness of God and has become a vessel of God's glory.

Arise, shine; for your light has come, and the glory of the Lord has risen upon you. For behold, darkness will cover the earth, and deep darkness the peoples; but the Lord will rise upon you, and His glory will appear upon you. And nations will come to your light, and kings to the brightness of your rising. Lift up your eyes round about, and see; THEY ALL GATHER TOGETHER, THEY COME TO YOU. Your sons will come from afar, and your daughters will be carried in the arms. Then you will see and be radiant, and your heart will thrill and rejoice; because the abundance of the sea will be turned to you, THE WEALTH OF THE NATIONS WILL COME TO YOU.

Isaiah 60:1-5
(NASB)

Notice the blessings are drawn to where the glory of God is seen. This glory can only manifest itself when righteousness has begun its transforming power in a child of God. This goes much further than simply being justified by grace. This righteousness that is by faith is our passport into heaven. But in order for the glory to exercise its power of attraction over all the blessings and attributes of the kingdom of heaven on this earth, righteousness needs to have removed iniquity from our being.

The glory of God differs from the anointing. The glory of God that immerses us in everything that is God is not a beautiful glitter that makes us feel good. The anointing is the ability to fill us with joy and love, but the glory is the consuming fire of God. The glory burns and destroys everything that separates us from God.

Many want the dimensions of His glory without ever having identified or uprooted the immense weight of iniquity within them. Prolonged suffering can be the result of approaching His glory in this manner.

Entering through the fire is a necessary step in the ways of God. Without His glory and righteousness, we can never possess our inheritance with blessings, found in His kingdom. First of all, iniquity must be identified and eliminated with, as a fundamental part of the victory in the cross.

Two virtues of the Almighty, righteousness and glory, are the very foundation of His kingdom. These virtues are not only going to polish us, but will also bring judgment upon our enemies.

> The Lord reigns; let the earth rejoice; let the many islands be glad. Clouds and thick darkness surround Him; righteousness and justice are the foundation of His throne. Fire goes before Him, and burns up His adversaries round about.
>
> *Psalm 97:1-3*
> *(NASB)*

It is important to understand that just as the love of God cannot stop loving, the righteousness of God cannot stop judging. In divine terms, God's judgments are sent in order to establish His righteousness. The Lord's judgments are lining things up with His perfect will and essence, and in this process He uses correcting judgments, revealing judgments and, in extreme cases, destructive judgments.

What does righteousness judge? It judges iniquity, as this is where everything that has been perverted from the ways of God is established. Wherever iniquity is found, we will find God's judgments in continual manifestation.

The same way in which righteousness and glory exercise a magnetic power over everything pertaining to the kingdom of God, iniquity exercises that same power, but with the opposite results. Iniquity will draw to itself, as if it were a magnet, everything that has to do with the empire of death and darkness.

Iniquity is the legal bases used by the devil to release evil upon the human being, and even more the believer. So you can see how important this topic is, as it is the bull's-eye for the devil's bombs and the bull's-eye for the judgments of God.

God Establishes His Righteousness with Mercy for Those Who Seek Him

The topic of God's judgments scares most people. It is wrong to think that every time God acts in this manner, something terrible is going to happen.

In my book, Seated in Heavenly Places, I discuss this matter. The first thing we must remember is God loves us deeply, and He is always thinking about what is best for His children. He desires for His glory and righteousness to be established in our lives. In this manner, all His blessings will come on us, and we will live in abundance, peace and joy, enjoying our beloved heavenly Father.

God acts through judgments of mercy upon those who fear Him and seek His righteousness.

I love them that love me; and those that seek me early shall find me. Riches and honor are with me; yea, durable riches and righteousness. My fruit is better than gold, yea, than fine gold; and my revenue than choice silver. I lead in the way of righteousness, in the midst of the paths of judgment: that I may cause those that love me to inherit substance; and I will fill their treasures.

Proverbs 8:17-21

My life was straightened out by God's judgments. Everything that was out of His perfect will was corrected with love. These judgments are designed from circumstances, words spoken in my life, dreams and moments of divine lucidity. The powerful work of God in our lives will establish us as "righteous" on the earth with all the privileges this affords.

There is a difference between being declared "righteous" by grace through the sacrifice of Jesus, and being established in righteousness. Blessings, honor and riches do not come flooding toward us after our baptism, but in the measure that we are rooted and grounded in righteousness.

King David clearly understood this principle, and he knew his victories depended upon the righteousness of God being established in him.

Arise, O Lord, in thine anger, lift up thyself because of the rage of mine enemies: and AWAKE FOR ME TO THE JUDGMENT THAT THOU HAST COMMANDED. The LORD shall judge the people: judge me, O LORD, according to my righteousness, and according to mine integrity that is in me. Oh let the wickedness of the wicked come to an end; but ESTABLISH THE JUST....

Psalm 7:6 and 8-9a

He also understood the judgments of God were sweet and wonderful, because they brought him closer to his beloved Lord.

When you love God with all your heart and strength, anything that hinders your communion with Him is unbearable, and you want it removed as soon as possible. There are things we are aware of and others that are hidden.

The statutes of the Lord are right, rejoicing the heart: the commandment of the Lord is pure, enlightening the eyes. The fear of the Lord is clean, enduring for ever: the judgments of the Lord are true and righteous altogether. MORE TO BE DESIRED ARE THEY THAN GOLD, yea, than much fine gold: sweeter also than honey and the honeycomb.

Psalm 19:8-10

God shows the prophet Malachi Jesus lovingly sitting and refining us. The Lord wants to do a perfect work in all of us. In order to do this perfect work, He must cleanse and polish us.

But who may abide the day of his coming? and who shall stand when he appeareth? For he is like a refiner's fire, and like fullers' soap: and he shall sit as a refiner and purifier of silver: and he shall purify the sons of

Levi, and purge them as gold and silver, that they may offer unto the LORD an offering in righteousness.

Malachi 3:2-3

The tribe of Levi represents the priesthood of His house, the holy priests that we all have been constituted by Jesus. The mere fact that He sits to refine us speaks to me of a work done with care, dedication and love. God purifies us in this manner, but not everyone has the love and meekness required, which allows this cleansing work to be accomplished.

God discipline others as a father corrects his children. And unfortunately, He will punish them to straighten out their behavior and save them from death.

It is impossible to have the blessings of God and to participate in His glory without the Lord first confronting our iniquity.

Conclusion

How Do We Deal With Iniquity?

We have seen throughout this book, iniquity is not just sin for which we ask forgiveness and that's it. Iniquity is the entire body of sin and evil, rooted within our spirit. Iniquity has corrupted the whole structure of our thoughts and our behavior. It has even infiltrated our bones and organs. Uprooting it takes time and dedication, but it will be the best investment of our lives.

The fruit of righteousness, together with the promises and the long-awaited blessings of God will manifest in us. A new chapter awaits, full of great joy and victory in Christ Jesus.

The first thing we do is asking the Holy Spirit to help us in this wonderful process of deliverance. He must send us a true spirit of repentance and the courage to change.

Pray this prayer with me or create your own that you can pray with sincerity:

Holy Spirit, I come to you today, humbling my heart, asking for a true spirit of repentance to come over me. Open my spiritual eyes so I can see my iniquity. Give me your gifts of revelation, dreams and words of knowledge, so I can understand my ancestors part that is affecting my life, bringing curses and obstacles that hinder me from living the life of abundance and blessing of Your kingdom.

Now, take a notebook in which to jot down everything that the Lord reminds you of or shows you.

Review the lists provided in the Bible as being iniquity. Pray over each of these sins, one at a time. Take a moment as you go over the list, waiting for the Spirit to bring conviction, memories or revelation. Then, confess your iniquity and the iniquity of your ancestors. It is likely that you have committed the same sins they committed, since this is recorded in your spiritual inheritance.

LETS BEGIN IN ISAIAH 59, THE MAIN CHAPTER ON INIQUITY:

- Hands stained with blood: Homicides, blood sacrifices (animal or human), love or participation in bullfights offered to virgins or idols, abortions, wars, genocide through conquering nations.

- Lying tongues: Religiosity, pagan religious practices, hypocrisy, all kinds of fraud or deceit.

- A wicked tongue: Slander, gossip, cussing, sarcasm, poisonous tongue, bearing false witness, murmuring.

- Not crying out for justice: Lack of compassion in the face of other's misfortune, indifference to the sins of cities, indifference to the sin of the church. We have the ability to do well, but don't do it.

- Not judging with truth: Making judgments from thin air, showing favoritism to those we love or those, which profit us. Showing favoritism to the rich over the poor. Racism.

- Trusting in vanity and speaking vanity: Trusting in riches, the system of this world, putting our trust in man, medicine, our salary, or the insurance of this world and talking about it.

- Thoughts of iniquity: Revenge, plotting evil, boycotting the work of God. All thoughts in which plans are constructed to do evil to someone else. Resentment and bitterness.

- Not walking in righteousness, via twisted paths: Trusting in our own righteousness instead of God's, taking the lordship of our lives, putting our decisions above those of God. Any road that does not lead to the righteousness, the will and peace of God is twisted. Not keeping a commitment, vow or promise, causing harm to others.

- Rebellion before God and His statutes.

- Departing from following God: Following and trusting in other gods, idolatry, occultism, witchcraft, divination, New Age, Satanism, spiritualism, sectarianism.

THIS IS THE LIST IN FOUND IN THE 10
COMMANDMENTS IN EXODUS 20:1-17 (excluding
those already mentioned).

- Taking the name of God in vain: Swearing by His
  name, using it without respect, as expressive exclama-
  tions. Telling jokes using His name. Blaspheming.

- Not resting: the non-Jewish Christian does not need
  to keep the Sabbath. Never the less resting in God is
  a way for us Christian to trust Him. In addition, not
  resting our bodies breaks a natural law of life. Stress
  and anxiety are iniquitous.

- Not honoring your father and mother: Lack of respect
  for authority. Speaking poorly about them. Not
  treating them with dignity and love.

- Committing adultery: Fornication, pornography,
  sexual perversion, unnatural, inappropriate use of the
  body or your spouse and all kinds of sexual aberration.
  Uncleanness, lasciviousness, orgies, impurity, unruly
  passions, incest.

- Stealing: Fraud, changing property boundaries with
  the intention of robbing. Falsifying measures, paying
  unjust salaries, tax evasion.

- Coveting: Your neighbor's spouse, his servants or his
  goods. Coveting the things of this world.

THIS IS THE LIST IN GALATIANS 5 (excluding
those already mentioned).

- Strife: Verbal or physical violence, enmity, arguing, jealousy, bad temper, dissentions. Anger, sowing discord, divisions.

- Heresy: Changing the context of the Word. Twisting Scripture in order to control and dominate people, intimidating them. Using the Word to obtain dishonest gain. Accommodating it in order to justify sin or lack of integrity.

- Drunkenness: Addiction to any drug, smoking.

- Envy: Wicked desires.

THIS IS THE LIST IN COLOSSIANS 3 (excluding those already mentioned).

- Greed: Trusting in riches. Indifference to the needs of the poor or the work of God. Idolatry to goods of this world (to possessions that can be "touched").

- Love of the world.

- Disobedience: To God, to His Word, to authority. Lack of submission. Rebellious, independent spirit.

THIS IS THE LIST IN 2 TIMOTHY 3: (excluding those already mentioned).

- Love of oneself: Loving "I", vanity, pride, haughtiness, and tyranny. Bragging, considering yourself superior to others. Conceit.

- Ungrateful: Feeling we are the owners of what we possess, without realizing that everything belongs to

God. Not living gratefully, and according to what Jesus did for us.

- Lacking in natural affection: Egotistical.

- Discontent: Never content, never satisfied with the good God gives.

- Intemperate.

- Merciless.

- Cruel: Sadistic, masochistic. Mental and verbal cruelty.

- Treason: Disloyalty.

- Loving pleasure more than God.

- Corruption: Conspiracy.

THIS IS A LIST OF OTHER SINS:

- Eating blood or drown animals: Eating cured meats made with blood or eating animals that have not been drained of blood.

- Tempting God: Criticizing God or accusing Him.

- Eating that which has been sacrificed to idols: Participating in pagan festivals in which food dedicated to idols is eaten, such as festivals for the dead, Halloween, saints or virgins.

- Profaning what is holy: Profaning our bodies, tattoos, body piercing.

- Prostitution: Selling oneself for money, selling principles for riches.

- Divorce. (Those not justified by fornication.)

- Homosexuality: Bisexuality.

- Sexual depravation: Bestiality (sex with animals), pedophilia (sex with children) necrophilia (sex with the dead).

- Unbelief: Distrustful hearts, double-minded, pessimism, faultfinding.

- Fear: Lack of faith.

- Forgetting the poor and widows.

- No fear of God.

- Usury: Lending money with interest or taking advantage of those who have borrowed money.

I have tried to make this list as extensive as possible in order to procure the greatest liberty. To me, there is nothing more wonderful than solving a mystery, and discovering something hindering my walk with God and then removing it.

As I have advised in previous chapters, at times it may be necessary to make detailed, exhaustive lists. This is not really a requirement for your salvation; it is for your total liberty and blessing. Once you have asked forgiveness very specifically, in each area, command all iniquity to be uprooted from your spirit and soul.

Then command the physical substance produced by iniquity be loosened from your bones and organs, and command it to exit your body. These are literal liquids, leaving the body; that manifest as diarrhea, vomiting, excessive urine, phlegm and runny nose as if one had a cold. This is perfectly natural and will leave in this manner.

It is a good idea when you are commanding these substances to exit your body, that you touch all of your joints and place your hands on the different body parts. If someone full of the Holy Spirit can help you, tell him to place his hands on each joint of the vertebrae in your back while you command the exit of iniquity.

You can pray something like this:

Lord, I ask you to forgive my iniquity and the iniquity of all of my ancestors. We have sinned against you. But today I repent for my entire ancestral line because we have committed...[such and such sin]. I ask you to forgive us and to cleanse me. Purge from my spirit, soul and body all iniquity.

I now command all iniquity residing in my bones and in my organs to exit my body right now. Iniquity, leave my bones and my organs in the name of Jesus!

Continue to do this until it manifests. It may take hours or even days for all of it to leave. You may feel a little tired. This is totally normal. You will recover quickly.

Once this is done, go on to cancel the curses that have resulted from the iniquity in your life.

Now you are ready for the righteousness of God to be established upon your life, and with it, all the blessings of God.

My Final Prayer for You

Father, I ask You, according to your mercy, righteousness and truth, to establish my brother (sister) in Your divine righteousness. From this day on, he (she) will be established as righteous, first of all by your selfless sacrifice, and secondly, because he (she) has departed from iniquity to follow your kingdom. I declare upon him (her) that all your blessings and your goodness will come upon him (her) and will overtake him (her). I declare that your mercy will rest upon his (her) generations.

> So shall they fear the name of the LORD from the west, and his glory from the rising of the sun. When the enemy shall come in like a flood, the Spirit of the LORD shall lift up a standard against him. And the Redeemer shall come to Zion, and unto them that turn from transgression in Jacob, saith the LORD. As for me, this is my covenant with them, saith the LORD; My spirit that is upon thee, and my words which I have put in thy mouth, shall not depart out of thy mouth, nor out of the mouth of thy seed, nor out of the mouth of thy seed's seed, saith the LORD, from henceforth and for ever.

Isaiah 59:19-21

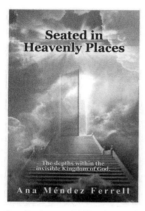